CHER

Design Renaissance

Selected papers from the
International Design Congress,
Glasgow, Scotland 1993

Edited by Jeremy Myerson

Open Eye

© 1994 Open Eye Publishing
in association with
The Chartered Society of Designers

Book designed by Barry O'Dwyer
and produced in Korea

Open Eye Publishing
18 City Business Centre
Brighton Road, Horsham
West Sussex RH13 5BA
England

Tel 0403 274598
Fax 0403 274599

ISBN 0 9516530 2 4

2

Contents

continued

Foreword

Stephen Hitchins
Chairman
Congress Steering Committee

This book brings together the leading contributors to the world design congress, Design Renaissance, which took place in Glasgow between 5-9 September 1993. More than 1,000 participants from throughout the world attended the event, organised by the Chartered Society of Designers, the professional body representing designers in the UK, on behalf of ICOGRADA, ICSID and IFI, the three international design organisations.

The overall theme of the congress was Renaissance – in the context of the urban environment, and the growth of new technologies for both products and communications, and in the light of ethical and political ideology. It takes more than a conference (or indeed a book), however successful, to achieve a Renaissance. Rather Design Renaissance was an exploration of the *potential* of the design process; of the progress that *could* be achieved. Perhaps the key message of the congress is that the responsibility for making such progress lies with the design community.

In this volume we have reproduced some of the broad ethical and political views presented at the conference, as well as more specialist contributions covering a wide range of design disciplines. Such a mix, it seems to me, accurately reflects the spirit of the debate engendered by the conference.

Design Renaissance owes a great debt to a great many. First and foremost to the City of Glasgow, which proved the perfect venue for an international design congress. In the last ten years, Glasgow has enjoyed a spectacular renaissance of its own – encompassing industrial growth, cultural regeneration, and many new and innovative design and architectural projects.

Particular thanks are due to the Glasgow Development Agency, Glasgow City Council and Strathclyde Region, to the Glasgow School of Art, Glasgow Museums and Galleries and the Design Council Scotland. The support from individuals within these organisations, notably Stuart Gulliver at the GDA, Dugald Cameron at the Glasgow School of Art, Julian Spalding, Director of Museums, Frank Binnie at the Design Council Scotland, the Rt Hon the Lord Provost of Glasgow, Robert Innes, and both the Convener, Strathclyde Regional Council, David M Sanderson and the Vice Convener, Councillor William Perry, was paramount.

I would also like to thank our sponsors – Philips Corporate Design, The China External Trade Development Council, Haworth UK, BT, BAA, the Stichting IKEA Foundation, the ICEP Portuguese Trade and Tourism Office and Andrew Muirhead & Son – whose support made the event possible.

Finally, this volume would not be complete without a thank-you to the individuals who organised such a successful event, Congress Director, Cherrill Scheer, Brian Lymbery, Director of the Chartered Society of Designers, and Jane Gray and Lynn Samson of Meeting Makers, the Glasgow-based firm of professional congress organisers.

This book will ensure that the valuable forum which took place in Glasgow reaches a new and wider audience. As such it is an important part of the task of both Design Renaissance, and the Chartered Society of Designers, to promote debate and discussion in all areas of the design profession.

Introduction

Jeremy Myerson EDITOR

The Design Renaissance congress at Glasgow represented a watershed in the way the international design community views itself. It marked a moment in time when designers and architects stopped showing each other pretty pictures of projects and started talking about the powerful and far-reaching contextual issues that will surround and shape their work in the future.

Speakers did not seduce their audiences with a portfolio parade of superficially reassuring images. Instead they used the congress platform to discuss a series of thoughtful and challenging ideas on how the design professions might usefully redefine their relationship with industry, society and culture. Design as object or product, fixed in time and space, was replaced by design as process – fluid, changing, perplexing, and increasingly unable to be contained by traditional disciplines or methodologies.

This book tries to capture that spirit of intellectual and philosophical enquiry – and encapsulate the strong feeling emerging from the congress that designers must move from the margins to centre stage in the political and ethical debate.

It sets out to bring the key debates of Design Renaissance to a far larger audience – to the tens of thousands of design professionals all over the world who must realign their education and practice frameworks in the face of a tidal wave of technological, economic, social and cultural change, and to the many adjacent professions that now touch design. The message of this book is also of importance to students of many fields whose task it will be to work within the multi-disciplinary contexts that lie ahead.

The wealth of material on which this publication draws is rich. Design Renaissance lasted for four full days and featured no less than 101 different speakers and papers from all over the world. Subjects ranged across the entire spectrum of artistic, scientific and human experience – from electric cars, intuitive robots and educational strategy to urban lighting, environmental problems and advertising photography.

Sifting through the tapes, transcripts and submitted texts of Design Renaissance revealed international perspectives on design of great breadth and depth. In selecting 30 essays for publication, I have sought to reflect the diversity of the views expressed while communicating the core concerns radiating from the congress.

What were these core concerns? This book is divided into five sections, each prefaced by a short introduction, in order to clarify them. The moral and ethical responsibilities of the design profession in a world now wracked by environmental fragility and economic instability proved to be the most powerful line of enquiry at Design Renaissance – and is discussed from many angles in Section 1. The crisis of the modern city – and the undermining of urban culture – also emerged as a key theme. Section 2 is devoted to the problems of urban decline and alienation and ways in which design can combat that.

Indeed a positive feature of Design Renaissance was that the congress showed concern to discuss solutions as well as dissect problems. New 'pathways' for design – fresh strategies, alliances and methodologies in relation to education, government and management – form the content of Section 3. Section 4, meanwhile, explores the future for product development in a world in which technology is now outpacing the ability of human perception to cope.

The final section returns to a broader focus with a collection of visions of the future on a wide range of topics. These are not utopian views, however. Indeed, as congress chairman Christopher Frayling points out in the book's Epilogue, utopia actually means 'of no place at all'. Rather, these are practical, hard-edged visions. Some – most notably the belief that the Detroit automobile industry will not roll over in the face of environmentalists, or that the design and architectural professions could merge totally within 25 years – may not be popular.

The writers in this book are among the world's outstanding design practitioners, theorists, academics and technologists. They have contributed their expertise from Europe (most notably France, Spain, Italy, Switzerland, Ireland and the UK), from North America, and from Japan. It has been a privilege to share their ideas and communicate their thoughts. I am also indebted to Paul Budd at the Chartered Society of Designers, to Barry O'Dwyer at Open Eye Publishing and to consultant editor Christine Atha for their work in preparing this unique compilation for publication.

Section 1:
The ethical dilemma

The single most powerful theme to emerge from the Design Renaissance congress concerned the ethical role and responsibilities of the design profession. This book starts, therefore, with a series of essays which address the fragility of the human condition and the different ways in which design can work towards healing serious fractures, not only in the environment but in the global economy. **Stefano Marzano** presents a political rallying cry for change to a profession metaphorically sipping chocolate for breakfast. **Erskine Childers** asks that designers use their powerful ability to influence perception to alert the world to the destabilising imbalance between rich and poor nations, just as they have already sounded the warning on the environment. **Victor Papanek** presents a scenario in which ecological and ethical considerations can provide the basis for an entirely new product aesthetic in the future. But this essentially optimistic vision is counterbalanced by **Ezio Manzini's** reflections on the meaning of social quality, in which he emphasises that radically different patterns of consumption can only be established via free consumer choice, not through a hair-shirted sense of ethical duty. **Tibor Kalman** too provides a counterblast to Erskine Childers' belief in the direct power of communication with a dark essay on photography, morality and manipulation in the media.

Chocolate for breakfast

Stefano Marzano ITALY/NETHERLANDS

Stefano Marzano received his doctorate in architecture from Milan Polytechnical Institute in 1978, and joined the Philips-Ire Design Centre in Eindhoven in the same year. He is now Senior Partner of Philips Corporate Design. He is also a Professor at the Domus Academy and lectures on design issues throughout the world.

Like the rich families of Europe, whose luxurious chocolate-eating idyll was shattered by war and social change, our industrial consumer societies are living on borrowed time. Racing against the environmental clock, designers must develop a political voice now – or they will have no say in the future.

I hope you had a good breakfast. I'd be surprised if you had chocolate for breakfast though. It is not everybody's taste. Some people – like me – even find bacon and eggs hard to take first thing in the morning. But a couple of centuries ago for rich families in Europe, it was very much the muesli of the day. It may seem quite far removed, but when I was thinking of the topic of designing for the twenty-first century, I was reminded of a poem by the Italian writer Guiseppe Parini called *Il Giorno*. It describes a day in the life of a well-to-do family, living a very comfortable life in a sheltered world, quite unconcerned about what conditions were like for those less fortunate than themselves. Of course, they had hot chocolate for breakfast. Theirs was a world of comfort and privilege. It was part of a western European idyll. One that was intensified by the Industrial Revolution, only to be finally shattered in 1914 when World War One broke out.

It was the world *par excellence* of *laissez-faire* capitalism, pursuit of profit, ruthless industrial competition and imperial adventures. It led directly to the Battle of the Somme and the futile horrors of trench-warfare. The subsequent imposition of impossibly heavy war reparations on Germany immediately sowed the seeds for World War Two, while the Russian revolution, a different reaction to unbridled privilege, contained the germ of the Cold War which was to follow three decades later. Now, the Iron Curtain has rusted away, and here we are witnessing in Eastern Europe the latest, but certainly not the last, link in a long chain reaction.

In the relatively comfortable setting of the industrial triad countries, such as North America, Western Europe, Japan and Australasia, we are metaphorically sipping our chocolate for breakfast. Meanwhile the masses outside begin, with increasing insistence, to knock on the door, demanding their fair share of the goodies we've been privileged to enjoy for so long. In other words, as we approach the millenium, we are being confronted with the effects of a gross imbalance in material circumstances around the world. Our idyll, our sheltered existence is beginning to crumble, and not only because we are being challenged by our fellow human beings, but also, of course, because our physical, natural environment is showing severe signs of strain.

Restoring the balance

If we are to look forward to a period in the future in which we have a stable environment and can pursue sustainable growth, then we must try to restore the balance in both these areas. Balance in our natural environment, and balance in our social and cultural environment. Are we doing enough to make sure that the world we'd like to live in will actually come about? A world where we not only have material comforts but a clear conscience as well. A world in which we can rejoice in the fulfilment of our own goals as well as those of others. The answer to this question is no, we are not doing enough. Let's just take a closer look at the sort of world we might like to see.

I have spoken before about a paradise regained. A world of 'happy objects and happy people', where people live at peace with each other and their environment. A world that is not static, however. Individuals continue to grow and achieve personal fulfilment. This paradise regained is, in fact, the world of sustainable growth. I have before sketched some ways in which designers can work, and indeed in some cases are already working, towards the realisation of this utopian state. I have stressed the need for a shift from quantity to quality.

But we are still living with the legacy of the Industrial Revolution, and the 'get-rich-quick' mentality, which brought the world of our chocolate-loving Italian family to such a bloody end. Manufacturers still compete very much on the basis of volume of sales and numbers of features. Many of the 'added extras' serve only as sales gimmicks of little or no practical value to users who become frustrated at the rate at which new models appear. No sooner have you got the machine home, than you hear of a new model about to be released which is, of course, bigger and better and, if you're unlucky, also cheaper. In the western world at least, the market is now becoming saturated. Clearly, this is not the way forward.

Quality products

Instead, we need to work towards quality. I know that's been said before. We're all familiar these days with the tenets of Total Quality Management. What I mean by quality is not that quantifiable objective quality which is the goal of TQM, but that less tangible, more subjective property which is so difficult to describe and yet so easy to recognise. In other words, a higher-quality quality. It's a pity we haven't yet developed a science of qualistics so that we could define it more precisely. We all, at least, know on a personal level as we grow older, that when it comes down to it, it is the quality of life such as time to spend with loved ones, or to explore interests or help others, that is important, more so than money and status symbols. A sustainable society requires this sort of mature outlook.

What does this mature quality mean in terms of consumer products? It means that products must become relevant to specific needs. We must not fall into the trap of designing products with more and more features which most people either simply can't understand or don't need anyway. What we can do instead is to give these products cultural significance or value for the user, so that they reflect personal identity. As designers, we can play a vital part in this. After all, design is in essence communication, and that includes the communication of cultural value and identity. To know what others want to communicate, we need to be sensitive to their concerns and reflect them in our designs. Form and function are not enough. Our designs must have content which is meaningful for the user.

If we do this, our products will also be ethical. They will truly reflect the user's own ethic, the ethos of his or her own individuality and personal ecology. By designing such relevant products, we shall ourselves be acting ethically, producing objects which enhance the consumer's quality of life.

Quality also means that a product must not disturb the balance in our ecosystem and harm the environment. We can ensure, for example, that production cycles are clean, economical with energy, and avoid dangerous waste. We can save resources by making products recyclable or last longer, or we can miniaturise them. We can shift the central essence of the product from hardware to the much more versatile software. These are steps that we, as designers, can work towards right now on what we might call the micro-level: the level of the individual design project within the individual company.

Society, government and design

The question is, however, is this enough? The answer again is no. The design community as a whole needs to start making its ideas and thoughts known on the macro-level. This is the level of government institutions, international organisations and society at large. Let's consider for a moment what is actually happening on the macro-level in relation to design. We don't need much more than a moment, in fact, as the role of government in design is minimal. Neither ministries of culture nor ministries of industry seem to see design as being within their domain. It falls between two stools. Most governments don't seem to see any connection at all between industrial policy and the cultural development of the people they're governing.

But design is a political act, and we need to become conscious of our political clout and significance. Every time we design a product, we are making a statement about the direction the world will move in. We therefore have to continually ask ourselves: is the product we are designing relevant? Is it environmentally responsible? The solutions we choose are political decisions, not design decisions. Design decisions belong in the sheltered world of chocolate breakfasts. Political decisions are steps out into the global arena. We must become aware of our power.

As individual designers it is, of course, difficult for us to influence the wider world. Understandably, people from other disciplines may not always share our views. Some may talk about higher sales, others about more functions. Not everyone approaches the problem from the same angle. I'm sure many of us, at one time or another, have felt we were knocking our heads against a brick wall in this regard. But the example of Greenpeace is instructive. Look at how this small group of determined people – we were inclined to call them fanatics until the hole in the ozone layer and Chernobyl proved them right – at least made us all aware that there was something wrong with the environment. I'm not suggesting we all race around in little rubber boats with Designpeace in big letters on the side, though I wouldn't stop anyone doing it if they felt it might help. No, what I mean is that we should not underestimate our power to lobby and persuade and cajole.

Why shouldn't ICSID, speaking on behalf of the design community at large, be represented on all sorts of bodies at all sorts of levels – corporate, regional, national, international – to explain how design factors play a vital part in affecting the quality of life. Unity creates strength, and, if our voice is to be heard above the clamour produced by proponents of the short-term economic quick-fix, it is strength on a global level that we need.

Accelerating change

Once the macro-framework of governments, corporate organisations and general public starts to understand the issues, this will inevitably trigger a snowball effect. Change will accelerate. Governments can establish industrial guidelines for maximising the relevance and cultural value of products, and they can develop ways of raising public awareness of such issues. Then, when we talk to colleagues from other disciplines, we'll be backed up by voices in high places, including that voice we'd all like to have backing us up – public opinion.

We need to demonstrate that industry and culture can mesh together in a mode of competition based not on quantity but on quality. We need to demonstrate that this is the blueprint for realistic sustainable development. And we need to do it quickly because we're involved in a race against the environmental clock. Look how unwilling some governments were to commit themselves to rapidly phasing out the use of CFCs. Even though we can all see, in those now-familiar computer pictures, how the ominously dark holes in the ozone layer continue to grow and grow. Changing people's minds and counterbalancing the attractions of short-term thinking take time. After all, the spirit of *laissez-faire* entrepreneurship which inspired the Industrial Revolution in the nineteenth century was alive and well in the west as recently as the 1980s under the names Thatcherism and Reaganomics. In other words, we shouldn't underestimate the deadweight of the status quo.

What we are fighting against is, if you like, the present-day equivalent of the myths, superstitions and power structures of the Middle Ages. We are, in fact, on the eve of what I call a new industrialised renaissance. This is a re-evaluation within our high-tech society of the human experience in its broadest sense, with genuinely relevant products meeting our true needs and aspirations, expanding our awareness and reach, deepening our understanding and power, expressing our identity. All within a healthy and sustainable natural, corporeal and manmade social environment.

The propagators of new humanist and liberating ideas half a millennium ago – people like Galileo, Luther and Erasmus – were not given an easy ride by the establishment. But if they hadn't taken a stand for what they believed in, much of what we have achieved over the last 500 years, imperfect as it may be, would not have been possible. Designing for the next millennium, designing for the new industrialised renaissance, demands that we in our turn take a stand right now for what we believe in. If we delay, if we are content to hesitate on the sidelines, we will be too late. We will just watch as our chocolate idyll disintegrates around us.

A programme of action
A few years ago, the British Design Council billed designers as 'The New Alchemists – adding the business ingredient that sends sales soaring'. But designers are not alchemists. Alchemy belongs to the Middle Ages, to the 'get-rich-quick' mentality. The riches we are after are less tangible than gold but of greater value. They won't come from some magic formula: we will have to work for them.

ICSID should resolve to change from an inward-looking talking shop to an outward-going politicised movement. One that actively works for the realisation of shared ideals. Within the framework of ICSID, we need to come up with specific political proposals for action. In global terms, the design community is a tiny group. If we are serious about designing for the next century, and indeed beyond, then we need an ambitious plan. If we aim our arrow at the church spire, we will be lucky if we hit the door. To stand a chance of reaching the spire, we must aim for the stars. In other words, we shall not have any effect on the next millenium if we limit ourselves to polite, or even heated, discussions every so often in interesting cities like Glasgow, stimulating though that may be. If we're to make sure that development is in a direction which takes account of our concerns, we will, like David, have to take up our sling – our political sling – and boldly go out to face Goliath. Potential planks in the design community's political platform include:

The environment
Obviously, environmental concerns should feature strongly, particularly in relation to the use of materials and recycling. But another more fundamental aspect of this, from which many of the specifics would follow, would be to emphasise where possible quality above quantity, so that we don't waste finite resources on unnecessary duplication or superfluity. I say, where possible, because while the industrial countries are experiencing excess quantity, the developing countries often do not have enough of the things that we take for granted. In other words, we need to argue for a sustainable balance to be established between quantity and quality in all parts of the world.

Economic imbalances

Western industrialised countries must look beyond their own sunny backyard and recognise the economic imbalances between north and south globally, between east and west in Europe, and, indeed, between the rich and poor within many industrialised nations. Given that these imbalances are threatening to result in a Cain and Abel situation, with us on the receiving end, there is all the more reason why we should try to find our way back into the Garden of Eden.

As long as the pure-profit quantity doctrine dominates, few will voluntarily undertake seemingly risky investments in poor countries. Yet such investment is absolutely necessary. I think we understand now that assistance should not all be in the form of hand-outs or loans from governments. This just results in more dependence. But if we leave everything to the laws of free-market economics, we shall have to wait forever before those countries are in a position to sustain their populations adequately on the basis of their economic activity.

Why not, then, some sort of positive discrimination? Companies could be encouraged to develop investment policies aimed at enhancing global sustainable development. Making products specifically geared to the needs and circumstances of developing countries, for example. Or investing on a quota basis in developing countries, just as in many societies, firms are encouraged or obliged to employ a minimum number of people from minority groups. Developing countries will be important markets for more sophisticated products later, but only if they've been able to develop in an economically and socially balanced way. If the world as a whole is to form a stable community of mutually sustaining trading nations, then it is in the interest of all of us that such balanced development is given a chance to take place.

Essential products and services

Who is going to make products or provide services which are not directly profitable, but which are nonetheless socially and economically necessary or desirable, such as public utilities and public transport, or the research phase of new technologies in universities or industry? State support or control of such activities has been tried in a number of countries this century. In most of them, this approach has been found wanting and they are being rapidly privatised again. Is this the right way forward? Or is it in fact a swing of the pendulum back to the past? Is there perhaps some other solution? Shouldn't we perhaps be moving towards a more global approach?

Certainly global agreements in a number of these areas could render investment less risky and therefore more attractive. Alternatively, some sort of globally-agreed levy imposed fairly worldwide could be used to support such activities wherever they were needed in the world, as part of a programme of what we might call 'world profit management'.

The benefits of such a programme wouldn't only be material. We designers would also have a professional interest in the maintenance of this sort of activity. Often enough, such activities ensure the continuation of poor or isolated communities, together with their unique cultures. Communities which might otherwise die, as younger inhabitants leave in search of comforts more readily available elsewhere. As each community and culture dies, human diversity is diminished. Look at how agricultural communities all over the world have abandoned the land for the bright lights, comforts, electricity, water and plumbing of the cities, only to end up living in squalor in violent shanty-towns. The current flood of refugees into the European Community and the USA from eastern Europe, Africa and southeast Asia is simply an updated version of the same story. Preserving human dignity and diversity is every bit as much a conservation issue as preserving pandas and rain-forests.

Countering unemployment

Many of the products we produce are responsible for putting people out of work. The march of technology inevitably brings pain with it, the pain of transition. Most western countries now have some way of alleviating the misery of being without work through unemployment benefits. During the past few years we have been able to see that this only solves a small part of the problem, providing the basic material needs. It does not address the frustration and damaged self-confidence which losing your job entails. A way to tackle this problem to maintain the quality of life is this: when developing a new product, companies should design not only the product itself but also a scenario of how the effects the product will have on people can be accommodated and positively exploited.

Companies will have to think ahead in socio-cultural terms, to beyond the moment of sale. What happens after the product has been sold should not be left to chance, but be designed. For example, if we're introducing a new automatic word-processing system, we should provide a scenario to take account of the fact that the machine will probably replace a secretary. The scenario might include the provision of training for the secretary so that that person can perform some new function for the company – an 'added value'. In other words, the manufacturers would not only be providing the hardware, but would also be providing an element of socio-cultural engineering. They would in fact be undertaking the conservation of human resources.

The result would be no victims, nobody being told that, as the latest euphemism has it, they are being 'given the chance to seek a new career opportunity elsewhere'. There would only be winners. In fact, governments might even be encouraged to make the provision of such a human-resources-conservation scenario obligatory. It would save the community the burden of paying unemployment benefits and it would maintain the dignity of people.

The rise of services

Designing such scenarios for new products is only part of a much larger trend away from the hardware aspects of products towards their function as the carrier of services. With the increased role of software in products and the need to conserve the material from which the hardware is built, this trend seems likely to continue. Upgrading software is more environmentally friendly than bringing out a new model, even if certain hardware elements of the product have been recycled. The next logical step in conserving materials would be for us not to own the hardware, but only to hire it when we need it. In other words, the centrality of the hardware, the traditional object-product, in the mind of the consumer will diminish, and the service will become paramount. The concept of property may even change. Designers will certainly find themselves being more designers of services than of objects.

The days when you could produce a pure techno-fix product and put it on the market without considering its potential implications for the world at large are over. Chernobyl saw to that. Our world is so fragile that we can't afford any more mistakes. We must get it right, more or less, the first time. This applies equally, if not more so, to the effect of products on people. We've worked out how to measure objective quality in products. Now we have to face the problem of measuring socio-cultural quality.

We used to have the impression that we were invulnerable. There was no limit to man's technological progress. But the hole in the ozone layer has shown us that our environment is under threat, and that we, too, are at risk. This realisation must surely lead to a new synergy, linking environmental conservation with the conservation of human socio-cultural values. We have lived a life of wild abandon, but we're now sobered as we notice the first symptons of debiiity creeping up on us.

Etica Nova revisited

At the ICSID conference in Ljubljana, I spoke of an *Etica Nova,* a new, universal ethic to underlie the design of objects. I see a politicised ICSID working to develop a specific code of ethics to guide designers, companies and governments so that choices can be made on an informed and responsible basis. I also see a series of alliances with other groups sharing similar goals. The green movement in its various forms would be an obvious partner. Consumer organisations might be another. We also need to enlist the media to our cause. This is crucial, because if the general public fails to appreciate the larger significance of our new type of product and continues to make choices on the same basis as in the past, then we shall not succeed. A sustainable development needs co-responsibility. The public need to be educated and the media can do that.

A proposal

Now, a very specific proposal. The British 'get down to brass tacks', the Americans 'get down to the nitty-gritty'. We Italians *veniamo al sodo,* we get down to the solid stuff. I propose that ICSID should set up a political programme panel. The task of this panel would be to draw up a comprehensive, practical code of ethics and to work out a coherent political platform based on that code. It would also explore the possibility of alliances with like-minded groups. I would suggest that the panel consist of up to nine members drawn both from the industrial countries and from other parts of the globe. The draft code and programme could then be put to the members of ICSID, discussed and voted on.

Some people may say to all this: we're designers, our business is designing, we're not politicians. To them I would reply that ultimately it is in our own interest, because if things continue along the present quantity-oriented path, in a saturated market there will be fewer jobs for designers. But we must also be in a position to see over our own garden wall, and put things into perspective. We must recognise that we are not merely technical operators but cultural operators as well, manipulating, expressing and delighting in human culture in all its diversity. We must grasp the responsibility and make our voice heard in the courts of the decision-makers.

Maybe we'll succeed in convincing them, or maybe we won't. But we have to try. What else can we do? Sit back and wait for someone else to say it all for us? If we do, we'll wait a long time.

I hope we shall decide to act, because, the very worst thing we could do is just go on sitting here. Just sipping away at our breakfast chocolate.

Chocolate for breakfast: complacent luxury of rich European families shattered by war and social change

Upbraiding the world to do better

Erskine Childers IRELAND

Erskine Childers was an independent writer and broadcaster before joining the United Nations. He has held many posts there including Director of the office of the Secretary General of the UN Conference on Technological Co-operation among Developing Countries, and Director of the Division of Information of the UN Development Programme. He has also been responsible for projects for the United Nations in Africa and Asia and is presently a Senior Consultant to the Governments of Denmark, Finland, Norway and Sweden for the Nordic UN Project.

Designers have played a key role in heightening perception of the fragility of the environment. Now they should use their communication skills to address the fragility of human society itself, in an unstable world wracked by war, starvation and gross material inequities between North and South.

The remarkable Marijke Singer – the former Secretary General of ICOGRADA to whom this memorial lecture is dedicated – described, in the words of Sidney Lewis, 'the state of the world as it is, then upbraided it for not being better'. That is exactly what we must do. But when we describe the world, we are using our *perceptions of it,* which are conditioned by the flows of information and the communication of stimuli which begin in the family, build in our school systems, move throughout our societies, and are reinforced by media of all kinds. And when we upbraid it for not being better, it is our perceptions that will determine whether we upbraid the right problems in the world, and upbraid the factors and leaderships in it that are especially responsible for it not being better. And because you in your various crafts are all intervening in the very *making* of human perception, I want to offer you some observations on the state of these processes.

It was only just over a century ago that Joseph Cowan dramatically declared in a House of Commons debate on the right of free speech, 'Information that was once the exclusive possession of a favoured few is now the common property of all. News of events that transpire at the other side of the globe and in our most distant dependencies is flashed here in a few hours. The world has become a vast whispering gallery.'

From that moment when the new telegraph had begun to accelerate and expand information flows, to our ability now to transmit any event from anywhere in picture and colour and real time through a billion television screens, what has been happening to perception of our world?

Various communication specialists have waxed enthusiastic about the so-called 'global village' and the marvellous advances that are being achieved through modern communication. I must submit to you that the overall results to date of these marvels gives cause for only guarded optimism, and little of that for the very part of the world that enjoys universal access to high-quality education and unprecedented wealth of information flows through modern technologies. The world I will sketch – the *real* world – is not the one being communicated to them. It is not the world that their leaders perceive; in fact they show every sign of wishing that real world would just go away.

Rethinking minorities

First, some fundamental facts that should underpin all such perception of our real world. We number five and a half billion people. Four out of five of us are *not* white, not Christian, not living in industrial urban societies, and not of western civilisation but of far older civilisations. And before I go any further, I have just included a phrase that tells a great deal about what goes on in minds filled with incomplete or distorted perceptions. I deliberately said that four out of five human beings alive are 'not white', because that is how most of the one-fifth minority still think of the majority – as minority. If those of us who have such pigmentation were capable of fully balanced perception we should call ourselves 'non-coloured', to distinguish ourselves from the vast majority of our fellow-human beings who are of colour.

When the Cold War apparently ended we witnessed another major fault in perceptions. The overwhelming body of media commentary and political utterance in the West said that the planet would henceforth be a far more tranquil place, which the so-called 'great powers' would now unite to police in what was proclaimed from Washington and echoed from London as 'the new world order'.

But the post-Cold War 'new order' doesn't seem to be working very well in any case, and the 'great powers' are showing, not unity, but inability to agree on almost anything involving the deaths of large numbers of human beings, even gender brutalities, ethnic cleansing, and genocide. The world of the 1990s is a far, far *more* dangerous place except, let us hope, in respect of nuclear incineration. This should not have been any surprise whatsoever. Extremely serious global problems inherited from the age of empires and the Industrial Revolution were suppressed from the perception for policitical purposes and because of the monumental distraction of the Cold War. Those legacies are now surfacing.

There is unprecedented restiveness among huge numbers of human beings all over the world. Transnational communication may spread the messages of the United Nations International Bill of Human Rights, but also the alluringly provocative myth of the affluent urban consumer life. Traditional nation-state structures are weakening everywhere, but with special likelihood of collapse of governance in cultures where the entire construct of such a centralist nation-state was imposed from outside.

Indigenous culture threatened

This is the United Nations Year of Indigenous Peoples and this involves yet another curious weakness of perception. One in every 18 human beings on our planet is a member of an indigenous people living in particularly harsh repression and erosion of their cultures and value-systems. One in every 18 of us. Read this slowly because it will astonish. All of this is part of an even larger perceptual problem which arose from a need to salve imperial pride; from the wish in major western centres of political and media power to make the historical fact of colonialism simply go away. Yet it had not in reality ended, for colonialism had placed the entire social evolution of *most of humankind* in stasis. It was like putting the great majority of human societies to sleep, halting their endogenous evolution of political institutions, and of attitudes towards and relationships with others, while a minority forged ahead with all such evolution.

Over *centuries* when no-one in what we now call the 'Third World' could form free political association and even discuss democracy, Westerners were increasingly free to do so; and yet a great many Westerners cannot perceive why Third World countries did not become exemplary copies of Parliamentary democracies within *a few years* of independence.

Again, in the centuries when Europeans were fighting out their own tribal wars, they prevented even that kind of evolution of relationships among their colonial subjects, and yet the fact of such conflicts now among groups in the Third World is widely perceived in the West as somehow connected with their cultures and colour.

Over centuries again, during which Europe and North America and Japan were building their public education systems, no such systems were *allowed* to be built among most of humankind. Ghana, for example, was released to independence in 1960 with a ratio of university graduates to total population which, if it had existed in Britain, would have provided the UK with only some 600 graduates for all purposes, or the whole of the United States with less than 3,000 graduates. Where would Britain and the USA be today? Yet after only 30 years there is impatience that developing countries still need assistance.

Haphazard decolonisation

When the imperial powers were finally compelled to yield, their decolonisation in the Third World was geographically haphazard so that their colonially imposed localities had to be accepted as in their boundaries partitionings. So not even then were these peoples, the great majority of all of us, really free to create their own neighbourships. The collapse of the Soviet empire has by contrast been so geographically synchronised that all the suppressed aspirations and ancient disputes put to sleep have erupted simultaneously – giving us a sort of instant-advance replay of the kind of trouble that has scarcely begun as yet across the externally imposed frontiers and partitionings of the South.

Then, too, the old imperial economic structure has never really been changed. The major industrial powers have actively prevented the UN from fulfilling its original, mandated role as the central forum for negotiating equitable and all-win macro-economic policies for the world as a whole. This began even before decolonisation. The loss of all stability in commodity prices, crippling the export potentials of non-oil producing countries and precipitating the OPEC reaction among the oil producers, began with the refusal of the USA to allow the establishment of the International Trade Organisation; and the manipulation of the International Monetary Fund from its original role as an equity mechanism between surplus as well as deficit countries is the other structural cause of the continued deterioration of the social and economic prospects of most of humankind.

Growing economic inequities

There are now severe and indeed potentially catastrophic economic inequities between the North and South, inequities which the G-7 powers have very largely ignored ever since the 1970s, but which have not conveniently gone away, only become steadily worse. In 1960 the richest one-fifth of the world's population enjoyed 30 times the income of the poorest fifth; by 1989 the richest fifth was receiving 60 times the income of the poorest.[1] Absolute poverty has increased by 40 per cent in only 115 years, to its present level of some 1.4 billion people – one in every four human beings alive. Let me say that again: as you read this, one in every four human beings alive is existing on the very margins of survival.

For accurate perception of our *real* world the ratio of 20:80, or worse, is very helpful because it dominates the planet today. As the 1990s opened, the 20 per cent Northern minority of humankind had 82.7 per cent of world gross national product; 81.2 per cent of world trade; had 94.6 per cent of all commercial lending; 80.6 per cent of all domestic savings; 80.5 per cent of all domestic investment, and 94 per cent of all research and development[2]. The 80 per cent majority of humanity in the South get the 20 per cent or less scraps from the tables of the affluent. Morality apart, this is not good business for the North, which will soon need new markets – but may find the majority of humankind not a market with purchasing power, but prostrate.

The South Commission, making a survey of the world as a whole and the place of most human beings within it, most significantly asked all of us to correct perceptions, to *recognise* something about our socio-economic disparities. Their report said: 'Were all humanity a single nation-state, the present North-South divide would make it an unviable, semi-feudal entity, split by internal conflicts. Its small part is advanced, prosperous, powerful; its much bigger part is underdeveloped, poor, powerless. A nation so divided within itself would be recognised as unstable. A world so divided should likewise be recognised as inherently unstable.'

False perceptions of the world

Ideologically driven reportage has been injecting another false perception against this one. It tries to suggest that all is well enough; that poverty is going to be defeated by 'the magic of the market', which it might be wise for us to perceive as a new fundamentalist religion whose icons are the keyboard and monitor screen and whose texts are the spreadsheets of hidden speculators who are allowed to trade away the very currency reserves of nations in seconds to the other side of the world, not for productive investment but for sheer personal profit. The magic of the market is not very well perceived by the bereaved of the 15 million rural poor who die every year of starvation and disease associated with malnutrition; or the 560 million rural wormen living in absolute poverty, 75 million of them the sole heads of rural households filled with 500 million old people and young children. But it is also not well perceived by such giants of the transnational corporative world as Akio Morita, chairman of Sony Corporation, who said in a recent open letter to the G-7, 'We need leadership to take us out of exchange rate anarchy, and toward some kind of sustainable order that will allow currency to play its true role in the international system: as a public-utility means of exchange for goods and services, not a commodity unto itself to be controlled for profit by a handful of speculators.'[3]

Thus, like a vast minefield buried under ice across the planet and now re-surfacing as the ice melts, these long-neglected legacies are producing more and more despair, anger and violence, even including vicious ethnic cleansing and tidal waves of displaced persons, currently totalling over 40 million, about one in every 135 human beings alive today. Some 36 major armed conflicts are today raging across a world which is littered with the most ghastly debris of the Cold War, the armaments of its protagonists, and is still being stalked by eager merchants of war.

Communicating root causes

What, therefore, can we identify about perception in this intensely troubled real world? First, I would suggest, it is clearly not enough merely to connect everyone with even live images of so much suffering and misery. More money may be raised for the outright humanitarian emergencies at the full *consequence* end of the spectrum, but more understanding of the *causes* and more concern to tackle them before they are transmuted into intractable and hideous effect does not at all seem to result from our unprecedented transnational communication. And as cause evolves into consequence, the cost in human lives and in money inexorably increases. This is morally outrageous and financially stupid, but communication has not yet enabled people to differentiate between consequence and root cause.

We have seen phenomenal, marvellous improvement in human perception of the fragility of our natural environment, not least thanks to the special sense of responsibility which the design profession has assumed in this. But it has to be significant, and troubling, that we cannot point to anything like the same improvement in perception of the fragility of our human *societies;* of the damage we are doing to our sisters and brothers.

War is not necessarily becoming regarded as more unacceptable by more people because it can now be brought live into their homes. In a brilliant exercise in mind-control, carried out by the very countries that claim to be the exemplars to the world of democracy, the Gulf War mesmorised most of western society like moths to bright television screens by a carefully orchestrated sanitisation of war into a sort of gigantic video arcade in everyone's living room, where the goodies zapped the baddies with high-tech weapons.

Decent western citizens were provided with the additional perception that a long-planned destruction, not only of military but of a developing country's entire basic civilian infrastructure – roads, bridges, water and sewerage supplies, electricity, warehouses of seeds for the next planting, laboratories that only made medical vaccines for human beings – that all this was merely 'collateral damage'.

Here, too, we witnessed the cumulative consequences of the longest fit of *suppressed* perception the western world has known – the suppression from its perceived history of the facts that Europe had to draw for the entire foundations of its brilliant advances upon the knowledge, in every discipline, that Arabs and Moslems had assembled from the whole Third World when it was the 'First World'. The very lens on the camera attached to the missiles that were seen in the global video arcade landing on Basra owed their origins to a brilliant Iraqi scientist of Basra, ibn al-Haytham, whose giant Thesaurus of Optics was still being annotated for its insights into perspective by Lorenzo Ghiberti as he crafted the reliefs for his Baptistry doors in Florence five hundred years later. But how many Westerners knew this, and could thus ponder its profound, poignant meaning?

I am indepted to Paul Rand, Professor Emeritus of Design at Yale University, for recalling the painter Robert Motherwell's perception of the quintessential roles of all you who are heirs to the Ghibertis and the al-Haythams. 'Most people', Motherwell said, 'ignorantly suppose that artists are the decorators of our human existence, the esthetes to whom the cultivated may turn when the real business of the day is done ... but far from being merely decorative, the artist's awareness is one of the few guardians of the inherent sanity and equilibrium of the human spirit that we have.' To awareness, I would add the artist's acute ability to perceive.

And so, I appeal to you as designers, you who are so incredibly powerful in what your crafts do, and can do, with human perception. Recognising all your constraints, especially all those of you who work in the marketplace, can you make it a point of honour to try to complement what you have helped achieve in guarding against damage to the environment, to communicate the importance of guarding against terminal damage to our very humanity?

Can you in your work find ways of strengthening the perception that we *are* one on this shrinking planet; that no culture and its adherents is going to conveniently get off it; that, as the South Report so cogently put it, a world so divided is dangerously unstable; and that the affluent minority must join with the impoverished majority in forging all-win, truly global economic strategies, lest in desperation and anger millions upon millions look at the world's centres of affluence and think about trecking or boating to them?

References

1. UNDP Human Development Report 1992 (Oxford University Press, Oxford/New York, 1992) pp34-36
2. UNDP Human Development Report 1992, op cit
3. Akio Morita, 'Towards A New World Economic Order', *Atlantic Monthly*, June 1993.

The coming of a new aesthetic: eco-logic, etho-logic, bio-logic

Victor Papanek USA

Born in Vienna, **Victor Papanek** is a working product designer with a background in architecture and anthropology, and is a well known writer. His special interest since 1963 has been design that is ecologically benign and socially responsible. He has worked for 30 years for the World Health Organisation, UNESCO and UNIDO. Papanek is the author of *Design for the Real World*, first published in 1967. His other writings include *Design for the Human Scale* and the forthcoming *The Green Imperative: Toward the Spiritual in Design and Architecture*

The industrial design profession is still treading water as it searches for a new aesthetic direction. But the needs of environment and ecology, underpinned by profound spiritual aspirations, could be a powerful influence on the look of things in the future.

'It may be that one has to choose between ethics and aesthetics, but whichever one chooses, one will always find the other at the end of the road.' – Jean-Luc Godard
'...We cannot remain moral in any recognizable sense of the word, nor can our projects and creations – including tools, homes, cities and landscapes – retain any sort of moral earnestness, without somewhere in the background the support of a deeply felt mythopedic or religious model of reality.' – Yi-Fu Tuan

There are seven points I wish to make. First, the sustainability of life on this planet – not just for humankind, but for all of our fellow species – is paramount. Even wars, with all their destructive power, usually can be absorbed environmentally. Two exceptions are the irresponsible mass-defoliation of the growing plant-mass in Vietnam by the United States, and the firing of oil wells by Iraq during the Gulf War.

Second, sustainability can be helped or hindered by design. I fully agree with Nicholas Freeling's observation that: 'An interest in cars is a classic sign of subnormal intelligence.'[1] Yet the impact of petrol-powered automobiles on the environment, wars, foreign policy, economics, morals and jobs is profound enough to serve as a chilling example.

Third, ethical design cannot exist if it isn't also environmentally sound and ecologically benign. It needs to be human and humane and embedded in social responsibility. Fourth, such design requires the help of governments, industry, entrepreneurs and laws. I began advocating this precisely 30 years ago[2], but much still needs to be done.

Fifth, we all seem to be treading water right now, waiting for some new style or direction to appear that will provide new meaning and new forms for the objects we create. What many of us are hoping for is a profound change in the way things look and work that is based on more than an arbitrarily invented style.

Sixth, assume that all objects, tools, graphics and dwellings must work toward the needs of the end-user on a more basic level than mere appearance or semiotic 'statements'. If this is true, then the lack of any spiritual basis for design makes ethical and environmental considerations mere afterthoughts.

Finally, I wish to show that when design is nourished by a deep spiritual concern for environment, people and planet, this moral and ethical standpoint will provide the new forms and expressions – the new aesthetic – we are all desperately trying to find.

Search for new directions

New directions in design always arise out of real changes in society, cultures and concepts. The sterility that still existed in household products, especially furniture and furnishings in the early 1970s, eventually led to a counter-revolutionary movement in the upper levels of the market. This movement in furniture design was comparable to Dadaism in painting, immediately after World War One. It resulted in chairs that could not be sat on, bookcases that could not hold books and other non-functioning devices. The clearest examples of this can be found in the witty and socially useful criticism exerted by Ettore Sottsass, the Memphis movement and others by objects designed to be of problematic use.

In an attempt to find still another new direction, the influence of the designer Luigi Colani has made itself strongly felt in the imposition of organic and fluid shapes in cameras, motorcycles, camcorders and many other objects. His published materials are a major influence combining ergonomic considerations with shapes that seem to have literally grown around the electronic and mechanical parts of a given object.

These same fluid forms next appeared on automobiles, with the justification that this new wave of streamlining – with 'spoilers' attached on the rear deck of the car – would make it more fuel efficient on the motorway. It is debatable whether the small amount of fuel saved in this matter (especially on cars moving at a snail's pace in heavy traffic) can justify the enormous energy and money wasted on redesigning and remaking body-forms. We are still, metaphorically speaking, treading water. We are still looking for a new reality-based aesthetic direction.

Search for the spiritual

Ecology and concern for the environment (which includes recycling, adaptive re-use, 'design for disassembly', the use of non-compound materials, and – most importantly – using less) are the most important and powerful forces to influence the shape of design. They may indeed develop the new directions that are so desperately needed both in design and architecture.

It is not difficult to find buildings that evoke the spiritual in us. The Ise Shrine in Japan, dating back nearly 700 years, Hassam Fathy's villages in southern Egypt built with the help of Nubian craftsmen, certain buildings by Pietro Belluschi, Frank Lloyd Wright, and especially recent works by Fay Jones come to mind. Many of these buildings are not religious in nature. Their designers had a profound recognition of rhythm, harmony, the Fibonacci series, and the eidetic image we carry through life – this infused them with spatial aspects that are transformative in nature and fill us with awe.

But design is different. At first sight, there is no such thing as a piece of industrial design that carries spiritual values. There can be no transcendental refrigerator, no righteous chair, or moral tea kettle. It is the *intent* of the designer, *the intended use,* the *fulfilled need* that can endow even the humblest object with deep ethical values. A chair is just a place to sit, yet a chair that is designed to enable a severely disabled child to find ease, becomes a moral device – with the designer reaching an inner state of grace through the act of helping others. A graphic design that enables a sick person to communicate symbolically with doctor or nurse, or empowers Inuit people to read books in their own language, a car that uses no petrol, lasts a long time and yet can be recycled easily – all these become spiritual through their ennobled function, growing the designer's soul.

Assemble for disassembly

Design For Disassembly (DFD) means that the product is designed to be easily taken apart, completely disassembled, and the constituent parts sorted for recycling. This implies simplifying parts and materials. The individual parts should be made of single materials rather than compounds since a mix of glass, metals, plastic, paint, shellacs and fillers on a motorcycle or car body makes the separating and sorting after use almost impossible and certainly prohibitively expensive. Design and manufacture for eventual snap-apart disassembly also influences fasteners and joining devices. Screws, glue and other mastic agents, as well as many welding and soldering methods, are out; two-way fasteners, pop-in pop-out rivets (as well as other joints still to be developed) are necessities.

Assemble for disassembly? Construct to destruct? It sounds odd, yet with curious concern for environment and ecology designing things to come apart efficiently is as important as to design them well initially. This approach may be obscurely troubling to some designers since it seems to put them into a double-bind. Their schooling and early work prepared them to design for obsolescence; that is, for frequent model-changes, fashion-oriented consumer products that would be discarded for the 'brand-new' latest incarnation of the same object, appliance or automobile, superficially tarted up to seem more desirable than last year's model.

Obviously both the number of electronic devices as well as the pace of marketing them has speeded up enormously during the profit-and-greed propelled 1980s – including the uselessness, triviality and vulgarity of many of these new products. Now in the nineties, these same designers, profoundly schooled in the design of the artifacts of a throw-away culture, find themselves facing a complete paradox: to design things that will last, yet come apart easily to be recycled and re-used. Yet the design profession – driven by new laws as well as necessity – is responding to the challenge.

Europe is decades ahead of the USA when it comes to eco-concern, and is also way ahead on design for disassembly. Electrolux of Sweden already has a DFD dishwasher, sold through Zanussi, its Italian subsidiary. But the leader of the disassembly initiative is BMW. The Z-1 two-seater has an all-plastic skin that can be disassembled from the metal chassis in less than 20 minutes. This $55,000 limited-production sports car has doors, bumpers and front rear and side panels made of a recyclable thermoplastic (a plastic that can be quickly and simply re-formed).

BMW also uses a pilot disassembly plant where it cuts apart five standard automobiles a day to learn new take-apart technologies. Some new lessons, such as substituting rivets and dowel-like connectors for glue or screws, are learned. Other approaches may be resuscitated from the past. The Citroen 2-CV of 1936 and 1948, and its many later descendants, was *bolted* together, without screws or glues. Other new insights tend to show that using scores at different types of plastic in manufacturing is wrong since it defeats attempts of sorting, and consequently prevents price-effective re-use. 'We have 20 different sorts of plastics in a typical car,' explains Arno Eisenhofer, BMW's disassembly director in Bavaria. 'Five kinds would be better and three should be possible.'[3]

Repairing rediscovered

One interesting insight, deriving from disassembly by BMW, is the rediscovery of repairability. In a seeming throwback to early Fords and other cars of the 1920s – when cars and everything else were built to be repaired – take-apart design makes it both faster and easier to work on cars once again. Trunk-lids, bumpers or doors can be removed without spending hours of labour-intensive, and hence costly time. David Thompkins, director of industrial design of a US manufacturer of engineering plastics owned by Montedison, a chemical super-corporation in Italy, says: 'When labour costs went up and material costs dropped, with injection moulding, automation and one-way fasteners we became a throw-away society. DFD is a way of re-thinking all that now'.

The German government has introduced new laws that will require its automobile makers Mercedes Benz, BMW, Porsche, Volkswagen and Audi, to re-buy, disassemble and recycle *all* German cars. Cars will be required to be made from non-compound materials, and specifically developed for easy take-apart.

This DFD technology has by now been adapted to large and small appliances and tools, down to the U-Kettle made by the Great British Teakettle Company. Yet the concept isn't all that new: the designer and teacher Jim Hennessey and I wrote a book in which we proposed design for disassembly and self-assembly for reasons of recycling as early as 1977.[4]

If the tool, appliance, object, or whatever, has been initially designed for take-apart technology to eventually result in easier sorting for recycling, then it

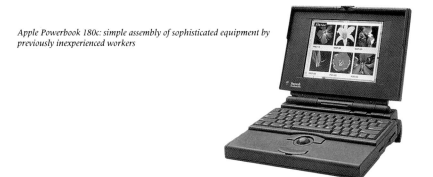

Apple Powerbook 180c: simple assembly of sophisticated equipment by previously inexperienced workers

should also be easier to assemble from discrete parts to start with. This insight can obviously lead to greater participation in the making process by some users, and this participation will, unavoidably, lead to a greater understanding on their part of the goods they have helped to put together. If we consider the British 'U Kettle' we realise that designing and making durable goods that can be easily disassembled, requires closer tolerances in connectors and joints, and less 'forgiving' parts. Satisfying both of these requirements, the teakettle is for these same reasons well within the ability of an average user to also build, or at least assemble. Again, we can recognise this approach propelling design toward a new aesthetic.

It is interesting to speculate about this new – yet unpredictable – look of things. Throughout history the appearance of built or made goods has been determined by what I have described as the function complex. To some degree the final appearance of a product or a dwelling has always reflected the personal gesture, whim or self-indulgence of the designer, as well as the stylistic mannerisms of the time.

Enough. The rise of a new aesthetic that is formed by environmental and ecological considerations will be unpredictable in its shapes, forms, colours, textures and varieties, and – at the same time – enormously exciting. Exciting since, unlike all new styles of the last hundred or so years, it will not be a manipulative re-statement of what has gone before. What, after all, was Post-Modernism, if not modern architecture with eclectic bits of kitsch added to hide the essential bankruptcy of both design and structure?

Keep in mind as well that I am not making a case for aesthetic transformation merely by extrapolating from a teakettle put together by someone in an evening. Industrial assembly procedures for most consumer products have become so simplified and made routinely easy that assembly work goes to the lowest entry-level workers with little or no experience and training. We can therefore expect that the number and types of objects people will be able to build for themselves will expand dramatically under the twin changes of manufacturers trying to simplify shipping and their own final assembly work, while take-apart design should also ease self-assembly.

None of this is really new – only the broad range and scale of goods will change. Washers, dryers, toasters, stoves, refrigerators, furniture, coffee makers, baby prams, wheelchairs, television sets, radios, steam irons, bath tubs, lamps, microscopes, exercising equipment, yes – even computers[5] – and much else will need to be redesigned for disassembly and could therefore at the same time be available as kits.

Nothing is simpler than to assemble any apparatus, machine or appliance. As I talk to you, sophisticated Macintosh powerbooks are hand-assembled by previously untrained workers in Ireland for the world market. Enormously complex Honda automobiles are put together by previously inexperienced ex-farmers and service personnel in Canada, the USA and Japan.

If one of the most important tasks of design lies in extending new options to the user, then it would be useful to make it possible for the average person to buy many of the things used at home or at work in one of three ways: the object in its fully assembled state; the object in kit form, to be completed by the user; and the object in kit form, to be assembled by someone else for the user.

This has in fact already happened in most parts of the world. It is no longer possible to buy a bicycle without assembling parts of it oneself. Most furniture is sold with the notation 'Some assembly required'. Without going into the economic benefits for the manufacturer of passing on some of the assembly process to the user, it is clear that the customer will learn more about the product, understand it better, and possibly be able to make simple repairs after having put it together himself or herself.

If one assumes a combination of design-for-assembly coupled to design-for-disassembly, one can see that this would influence the aesthetics, the look of things and become a powerful modifier of appearance. And it would be largely propelled by the needs of ecology and environment, as well as an underpinning of profound spiritual aspirations.

References

1. Nicholas Freeling, *Castang's City* Heinemann, London 1980.
2. Victor Papanek, 'Areas of Attack for Product Designers' in *Journal of the Industrial Design Education Association,* New York, April 1963. Published in expanded form as *Miljon och Miljonerna,* Stockholm, Bonniers 1968 and as *Design for the Real World: Human Ecology and Social Change,* London and New York, Pantheon Books and Thames and Hudson 1970.
3. Quoted in the article 'Built to Last – Until It's Time To Take It Apart' by Bruce Nussbaum and John Templeman, *Business Week,* 17 September 1990.
4. Victor Papanek and James Hennessey, *How Things Don't Work,* Pantheon, New York, 1970
5. One can see that turning the making into sell-making, especially in the case of sophisticated devices, will call for the introduction of many diagnostic devices to the user market, as well as built-in auto-diagnostic devices in many goods. This has already started with elaborate built-in virus detection and cleansing programmes in Apple Macintosh computers.

Design, environment and social quality

Ezio Manzini ITALY

Ezio Manzini is Director of Design at the Domus Academy, Milan and Associate Professor of Architectural Technology at the Polytechnic of Milan. He has undertaken research into new materials and interactive objects in collaboration with companies such as Philips and Kartell. His publications include the influential book, *The Material of Invention*, first published in 1986. He lectures frequently on design throughout the world.

Environmental awareness has moved from the margins to the mainstream, yet the issue has been 'normalised' within existing patterns of production. Now the challenge for designers is to create products and services which encourage a radically new style of consumption based on social quality.

The environmental issue has a lengthy history. In 30 years it has progressed from being an agitated debate amongst scientists and highly aware pressure groups, to become a theme that touches the whole of our society. It has come to have an influence so pervasive that it affects both generalised global trends and simple everyday decisions.

During the course of this history at least two decisive changes in perspective have become necessary. The first is a shift in emphasis. This has changed the environmental issue from a minority cause to a problem formally acknowledged and adopted by us all. The second shift in perspective must take place today. It should lead to a vision of the environmental issue as an integral part of a larger phenomenon. This is the complete crisis of the development model which has been dominant in society until today. With this new perspective on the environmental issue it is possible to make proposals which advocate the necessity for a much more radical approach in dealing with the interaction of design and sustainability.

The 1980s: normalised ecological design

During the past decade the environmental issue has penetrated mature industrial societies like those of the USA and Europe, affecting their various 'social actors' in different ways. It has led to new policies, become an integral part of corporate programmes, and introduced a new demand for environmental quality in the marketplace. Thus an *ecological* re-orientation of the systems of production and consumption has become a widely discussed and widely accepted theme.

Nevertheless, because this debate took place during the 1980s, it did so in the context of an industrialised society in which the world appeared to be wealthy, healthy and satisfied. From that viewpoint the environmental re-orientation of the system would not require difficult changes in lifestyles nor, in any case, changes in the overall way of doing things. It was imagined simply as a series of operations to be effected within what was fundamentally accepted as a stable social and industrial framework.

In this kind of cultural atmosphere, the environmental issue has tended to be viewed as a political, economic and engineering problem to be treated in a purely technical manner. Therefore, through an appropriate redesign of what is already here, we solve the problem. The fact that CFC is removed from spray cans, that park benches are made of recycled plastic and that automobile bumpers can be removed and recycled means that we are dealing with these issues.

All of this is important, and its significance should not be underestimated. The fact that it has become normal to think that these things should be redesigned in order to render them less harmful to the environment is clearly a noteworthy achievement. All possible efforts should be made to ensure that the acceptance of this principle is translated into coherent practice to the fullest extent. However, the inadequacy of this 'normalised' way of dealing with the environmental question is becoming increasingly evident today.

The 1990s: from 'normalisation' to a new radicalism

Today the environmental issue begins to look more and more like a part of other much larger themes. What has gradually emerged during the 1990s is that there is a significant interweaving of social, economic, political and ethnic questions at an international level. This has led to the widespread sensation, even in the most industrialised nations, that what is taking place today is actually a structural crisis. The global model of development is the true issue under discussion. This general background is important, because it is from this starting point that it becomes possible to view the environmental question and its relationship to design in a new light.

Faced with the evidence of the connection between these environmental, economic and socio-cultural crises, it becomes increasingly clear that the scenario of the redesign of what exists is not sufficient to substantially address the real issues. Such a path will lead to a system of production and consumption which is less polluting than the present one, but which cannot be considered sustainable over the long term. This is becoming increasingly obvious to those who work closely on environmental questions.

So even though a recyclable motorcar is better than a traditional one, it makes no contribution to resolving the problems of urban mobility nor the problems of unemployment, nor that of the conflicts between the North and South of the globe. There is a conviction emerging among many social observers that existing products are inevitably destined to change because of these other crises impacting upon them.

What is really required today is to imagine truly innovative solutions. This means products with a high level of radicalness. These are products which contain some kind of hypothetical response to the problems at hand proposing alternative paths to those of the past and present. This objective might appear rather ambitious. But it is justifiably so. The aim is not to find the one and only solution for all questions. The idea, more modestly, is to propose solutions which contain some spark of innovation, where innovation means a new way of behaving or of viewing the world.

This new model of development will not be born on a drawing board, or around a conference table as a perfectly complete theorem. It will emerge from dialogue and conflict among a multiplicity of ideas, visions and proposals. It will come into being thanks to a widespread atmosphere of innovation involving all those active in society. Therefore designers will undoubtedly play a part in the process.

Environmental policy: tactics and strategy

That this entire scenario is problematic is obvious. However let's consider the parts most closely linked to the activities of the designer. These are the products, services and, in wider terms, the criteria of quality and value with which we evaluate the artificial environment.

Considering this theme from the point of view of environmental sustainability, it becomes obvious that we must pursue the objective of a society in which there are different lifestyles. These would be lifestyles based as little as possible upon the consumption of energy or materials, or other resources such as land, air and water. Clearly this objective can take on a variety of meanings, and can be pursued with different environmental policies in keeping with different possible interpretations.

Environmental impact is the result of a population which 'demands results' and the specific impact of the technologies employed to achieve those results. We can consider an environmental policy as *tactical* when, supposing that the results cannot be modified, one attempts to improve the technical eco-efficiency of the system. This is realised by improving the technologies employed to achieve the results. Following this path, changes in lifestyle are not required, and the role of design is that of effecting redesign of the existing products.

On the other hand, it is possible to consider an environmental policy with a *strategic* effect which, placing the social demand for results in discussion, seeks to achieve a higher social eco-efficiency. In other words, an improved relationship between the individuals to be satisfied and their demands for results. In relation to the available technologies. To make an environmental policy of this kind practicable it is necessary that significant changes in lifestyle take place. This along with socio-cultural innovation could lead to completely new consumption scenarios.

Consumption scenarios

First, from consumption to care: this scenario implies going beyond the misunderstood notion of the functional which has led to the acceleration of consumption and to the world of disposable objects. Here, design will have to develop products with the technical and also the cultural capacity to survive over time. These will be products which require care and with which the user can establish an emotional relationship.

Second, from consumption (of products) to utilisation (of services): this scenario implies going beyond the notion of possession and, therefore, of personal consumption of products. Instead it looks for a concept of utilisation which is that of a non-destructive and non-individual consumption of products and services. This is a scenario in which a higher level of social eco-efficiency can be achieved by orienting the demand for results toward new services which offer high efficiency in terms of the use of resources. In this context, the task of the designer will be that of developing products and services with high environmental potential and, at the same time, a high level of social approval and attraction.

The third scenario is from consumption to non consumption. This scenario is obviously the most radical as it can only take place at a cultural level. In this context, design, viewed as the culture of products and services, can play an important part. Design can generate scenarios, criteria of quality and value judgments in which the reduction of needs can be experienced as an increase in social quality.

Cultures of reduction

All this may remind us of certain experiences of the past. The pursuit of an *existenz minimum* during the first decades of this century in Europe for example, or the anti-consumption phases of the 1960s in Europe and the United States. Undoubtedly links of continuity do exist with these movements but it is more useful to point out the differences. In different forms, the two movements mentioned above sprang from motivations of an ethical nature. They were in opposition to a model of production and consumption which was in an early phase of development or at a high point in its development.

The ethical force of the present situation, on the other hand, has a much more concrete and tangible basis. It challenges a mode of consumption which is visibly destined to change because it is based on a mode of development which is deeply in crisis. If we examine the situation from the point of view of the designer, the problem is not so much that of evoking an ethical principle based on an environmental necessity. It is more one of proposing solutions which appear to be better than those presently in use. Today's *existenz minimum* must be translated into proposals which can appear, to increasingly large segments of the population, as opportunities to achieve a higher level of social quality. This must equate with quality of life. However, in doing so we must eliminate the individualistic, hedonistic connotations which have been attached to this expression. A possible slogan might be *existenz minimum* as *maximum quality.*

Existenz minimum? Maximum quality!

The problem for designers can be summed up as follows. How can we propose an *existenz minimum* which will appear attractive enough to be freely chosen in the midst of a variety of alternative proposals. First of all, in order to be attractive the proposal must not correspond to a scenario of deprivation. This is a notion of life which exists within the same values and criteria of quality as those of the past but which offers a little bit less of everything. It is a world in which the expectations of quality remain the same, but which instead offers fewer automobiles, less lighting, fewer disposable products or fewer strawberries in December. Such a world could only come into being as a necessary response to some sort of catastrophic events. It is unthinkable as a product of free choice.

Fewer motorcars, fewer disposable products, less exotic fruit are factors which can not only become acceptable, but even attractive. However it can only do so within the framework of a new cultural scenario. This is a scenario in which cars are no longer as necessary because there are other, better ways of moving about. It is a scenario in which to rediscover the value of care for material things and the quality of things and the quality of things to be cared for. It is a culture which appreciates a sense of the passage of time and the changing of the seasons which is communicated by the variations in the fruit available for consumption.

Design can play a fundamental role in the definition of many such scenarios which, in a complementary or competitive manner, lead in this direction. In order to do so, design will have to re-examine the very basis of its culture. It should not be forgotten that design was born and developed within the context of the development model in crisis today. Fundamental concepts such as form, function, client, user, market must be revisited. The same is true for the role of technology, aesthetics and design itself.

Technology: tools for new types of behaviour

Over the years technology has been a powerful force for change. This is not only because of the emerging evidence of the environmental problems caused by its employment, but also because of its destabilising influence at a social and cultural level. Our concepts of space and time have been transformed by telecommunications and those of matter changed by new materials. The notion of work has been redefined by automation, those of reality changed by the advent of virtual realities, and those of life altered by the possibilities of genetic engineering.

The real problem today is that of how to direct the present power of technology towards the needs of sustainable society and of a coherent model of development. The sustainable society requires products and services which make use of new technologies for the care of things, for intelligent participation and for a new social quality. But the problem is also that of understanding how to transform this technical apparatus. We must remain aware that this apparatus has already transformed us, and has transformed what we think of as our environment.

Aesthetics: giving form to sustainability

Every era has its own ethics and its own aesthetics. Aesthetics represent the way in which a historical period and the values it contains take form. During the first part of the century, design played a decisive role in giving form to modernity. During the 1980s, for better or worse, design was the protagonist of an aestheticisation, as superficial as it was widespread, of things. This aestheticisation, on the whole, has proven incapable of countering the more generalised aesthetic decay of the world. Today, the perspective of an sustainable society has not yet taken form. The aesthetic of sustainability has yet to be born.

This problem must be considered very seriously. There is a widespread belief that the aesthetic dimension is a secondary one. It is an extra to be added when the rest has been resolved or a luxury for those who have everything. This leads to the impression of a sort of contradiction between ethics, with its presumed rigour, and aesthetics with its presumed frivolity. It should be clearly stated that this opposition is typical of the 1980s and the cultural confusion of that period. In reality, aesthetics is connected to ethics in the sense that no true, profound aesthetic renewal can take place without being based on a value system.

In a phase of transition such as that of the present, this aesthetic dimension becomes a fundamental factor for change. It becomes a social attractor, in the sense that it orients the choices of a multiplicity of individuals. It becomes a way of expressing in a synthetic, and therefore intelligible form, the complexity of a proposal. In summary, at the present moment we can state that the perspective of the sustainable society has a great need for an aesthetic of sustainability.

Design: giving form and offering opportunity

Design certainly cannot change the world, nor can it design lifestyles. It cannot impose ways of acting on people in keeping with its intentions. But design can give form to a changing world, and offer opportunities for new types of behaviour. To *give form* means to operate within a more general cultural context. This means amplifying and rendering visible the weak signs expressed by society in terms of new types of demand and of behaviour. It also means proposing consistent criteria of quality from a perspective of sustainability and designing overall scenarios which *give form* to the sustainable society.

To offer opportunity means acting in the field of direct intervention. It means proposing products and services which make possibilities concrete, which offer opportunities for new types of behaviour and new lifestyles in keeping with a new notion of social quality. These are the areas in which design can play a significant role in the social dynamics of the period to come. These are the limits of its action, but they are also its possibilities and responsibilities. These themes will constitute the terrain upon which the hopes for the achievement of a new, sustainable society will or will not be realised. It will be realised not by necessity or by imposition, but through the free choice of solutions judged to be improvements. The aftermath of the present model of development may eventually assume many forms. The one which is the result of a free choice of solutions, evaluated and understood to be better, is certainly the most auspicious.

Photography, morality and Benetton

Tibor Kalman USA/ITALY

Tibor Kalman was born in Budapest and grew up in New York. He recently closed his highly successful design studio M&Co to pursue independent projects in publishing, industrial design, video design and production. Kalman edits *Colors*, a worldwide multi-cultural magazine sponsored by Benetton. M&Co clients included Talking Heads, Knoll, Formica and Chiat/Day.

Worldwide controversy over the Benetton advertising campaign which uses powerful social imagery to sell jumpers has fuelled the debate over the 'honesty' of photography. But the photograph is no more 'objective' than painting and can lie just as effectively. The only option is for people not to believe the media.

I currently edit *Colors,* an international magazine sponsored by Benetton. It is a multi-lingual magazine pairing English variously with French, German, Italian, Spanish and Korean. *Colors* takes outside advertising and its format changes from issue to issue. One of its fundamental aims is to challenge assumptions about what a magazine can be. Benetton funds *Colors* without exercising control over its contents.

Benetton, of course, is the company that has generated worldwide controversy by using emotionally-charged imagery in its own advertising. Charges of intrusion, cynicism, inappropriateness and bad taste abound. Central to the controversy is the issue of the nature of photography. The moral questions often arise out of people's belief that Benetton is using 'real' photographs for 'unreal' advertising purposes.

Whatever Benetton's motives, I believe that this whole question of some photography being 'true' and some 'untrue' is a non-question. Photography is not objective; it never was objective. It has never told the truth any more than any other form of artistic communication can. In the first days of cinema, people ran from the movie theatres thinking the train on the screen was going to come crashing out into the audience; more recently some people were scared of the monsters in *Jurassic Park*.

Early in the history of photography models were used to enact situations for a camera to record. Later, we learned how to retouch images, first by hand, later by rearranging the tiny dots that make up the images. Meanwhile, there has always been the cheapest and easiest way of making photographs lie – simply changing the caption to change the meaning of the image.

Some people accept this but still argue that the photograph remains in some way uniquely 'honest'. They say that for it to exist, some kind of real-life situation also had to exist. They claim that the fact that a camera can be set up by remote control to record whatever passes in front of it somehow confers objectivity. They cling to the idea that the photograph is an inherently 'real' or honest image and as such is always on a different plane from an obviously subjective form of visual communication such as painting.

However, I believe that photography is just like painting and that it can lie just as effectively. I do not accept that there is necessarily a 'true' moment that the camera captures, because that moment can be manipulated as much as anything else.

A question of context

That argument is really a diversion from the real issue, which I believe to be one of context – the way we react to images presented in different contexts such as editorial or advertising. Literal-minded people say 'we must legislate' and that there is a need for some code that newspapers and television should obey to prevent them from manipulating readers and viewers with images wilfully used out of context. This is impossible. You simply cannot pass a law that says magazine editors or reporters cannot lie. Instead you have to learn (and then to teach others) to mistrust everything.

The development of new and sophisticated retouching techniques has intensified the debate about how 'real' photography is. This is a good thing because it highlights the fact that photography can never be objective. Photography should always be questioned the way all kinds of authority should be questioned.

The Benetton campaign

So how do we educate everyone into questioning the images they are constantly bombarded with by billboards, books, newspapers, TV, movies and magazines? One way to approach the Benetton campaign is to allow that it may have an educational contribution to make. Instead of accusing Benetton of trying to sell sweaters with images of human suffering, think of their advertising as an exercise in challenging assumptions and raising issues: a media experiment sponsored by a clothing company.

Consider the famous Benetton example of the new-born baby that appeared on billboards and the cover of the first issue of *Colors*. If we had been photographing this baby for a pretty mums' magazine, we would have cleaned the baby with retouching. Instead we chose not to. This is an example of contextualisation. In the first place, Benetton paid for a photograph from a news organisation. They then re-contextualised it into an advertisement. Then – for the cover of *Colors* – we re-contextualised it back to editorial again.

An even more controversial Benetton image was that of the dying AIDS victim. Here I believe what Benetton thinks it is doing is sponsoring education by raising social issues. However, one incontrovertible result of that poster is that there has been widespread discussion about it. In the press that discussion has been negative and concerned with the assumed objective of selling sweaters in a dubious way. However, among the public the real subject of discussion has been the picture itself, and the unsettling implications of using that sort of image in an unfamiliar context.

A healthy scepticism

I am not an apologist for Benetton, but I do think that we should value anything that encourages us not to believe pictures and not to believe the media. The media are subject to manipulation by the police. They are subject to manipulation by corporations. And of course they are subject to manipulation by Benetton. What those of us who work in the media have to do is to self-destruct and tell people not to believe us. In the final analysis, it is the only honest course open to us.

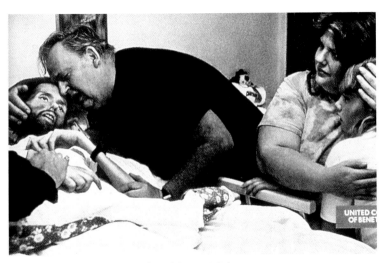

Controversial Benetton advertisement shows dying AIDS victim:

Section 2:
Culture and the city

A recurring theme of the Congress was the idea that the city has descended into crisis – that the fabric of the urban environment is in danger of disintegrating, along with the social codes that bind communities together. Designers of all disciplines have a role to play in maintaining the delicate balance of buildings, communications, systems, products and infrastructures which make our cities function – not just in technical terms but in cultural ones too. The essays in this section explore the nature of the cultural threats to the city, from an eloquent attack on the growing fragmentation and banality of French cities by **Jean Claude Garcias** to **John Worthington's** analysis of the decline of the public realm and community values in British urban life. **Rodney Fitch** reflects on the impact of the US-style shopping mall on the dynamics of local cultural identity. But the city is not beyond redemption and regeneration, as our essayists demonstrate. **Stuart Gulliver** explains what Glasgow – a model city of urban renaissance – has already achieved and what it plans to achieve in the future, while fellow Glaswegian **Janice Kirkpatrick** outlines the specific contribution designers can make in managing urban cultural strategies. Remodelled cities, of course, demand new design skills. These range from the skills of the urban scenographer, suggested by Tudor Vdelatan as a way to transform the night image of the city for commercial and cultural benefit, to those of the architectural producer, credited by **Sy Chen** with bringing a new international perspective to Japan's information-overloaded built environment.

France's changing cities

Jean Claude Garcias FRANCE

Jean Claude Garcias is Professor of the History of Architecture and Town Planning at Paris-VIII-Vincennes University in France. He is also a critic and practising architect. With the practice Treuttel-Garcias-Treutal he has designed several low cost housing schemes in the Paris area. He has a monthly column in *Bulletin d'Informations Architecturales,* the journal of the state-sponsored architecture centre, the IFA.

French cities are changing – but are they changing for the better? Increasing segregation and fragmentation along race and class lines, allied to grandiloquent, media-minded architectural projects by despotic local majors, suggest they are not.

I shall begin in a slightly negative way, stating what my paper won't be about. It won't be about cities 'as they ought to be', from an aesthetic, social or political point of view; what could be called the model city, or the *News from Nowhere* syndrome. More than a century ago William Morris honestly tried to describe the good city of the future, and he honestly failed.

Dozens of architects, or self-appointed theorists, planners or reformers have tried since, sometimes with less honesty, in the name of progress, science, the dictatorship of the machine, hygiene, social utopia, you name it. One need only mention E Howard, Frank Lloyd Wright, Sant 'Elia, Mies Van de Rohe, Le Corbusier, Buckminster Fuller or Yona Friedman. They were all convinced, one hopes, that *their* way of designing cities would on the whole solve the problems of mankind. And if architects are so numerous among would-be changers of cities, the reason is they are often consenting victims to that occupational hazard: prophesying. They like to prophesy happy, modern days to come. The current state of those parts of our cities built according to debased modern plans should incite more to modesty.

So my paper won't be about cities 'as I would like them to be'. I'm not trying to convince 'Authority', as Corb would say, of the soundness of my private and selfish plans. Yet I cannot refrain from expressing a taste for compact cities, where people live, work, meet, and even fight; cities whose users and consumers are also the inhabitants and the keepers; and not only harried commuters or hordes of bemused tourists; cities where the coherence of lives and the beauty of the streets are given more importance than the efficiency of 'networks'; cities where the permanence of human habits and the perennity of buildings are valued above speed and transparency.

To quote a few statistics. In my hometown Paris, inside the ringroad, with a population of two million, everyday 400,000 lucky people go to work in the *arrondissement* or borough where they live; 400,000 in another borough but inside the ringroad; and 200,000 have to cross the ringroad.

On the other hand, one million people from the suburbs enter the city every day, and 100,000 from the provinces. The process is repeated in reverse at night.

Such a situation is conducive neither to urbanity, nor local democracy, nor even civil peace. I hear that an English prince and an architect from Luxembourg have formed a partnership to return to good urban design, to the vernacular, to the models of the past. I don't think they can succeed, as neither nostalgia nor enlightened despotism can change the city. But I understand the mass support they enjoy, especially when they lash out at so-called modern architecture.

Questioning the culture of congestion

I won't discuss cities 'as they will necessarily become', that is according to the liberal creed, however cleverly masked by the likes of Rem Koolhaas or deconstructionists. The cities of *laissez-faire* and chaos, of 'park and ride' or expressways leading nowhere, the 'non-clustered cities' modelled after Atlanta or Osaka. I've always had doubts about the validity of 'the culture of congestion' or the surprising beauty which is born of an excess of hideousness, or the necessity of the tall office building in the European context or skyline.

Besides, if the invisible hand also regulates the design of cities, what need is there for architects and urban designers? Five years ago the city of Lille in the north of France decided to give deconstruction a chance, or to put the theory of architectural chaos into practice. We shall soon be able to judge the results; particularly the relevance of skyscrapers on top of a high-speed train station in a city which abounds in vacant lots.

My paper won't be about French cities as they are, or rather as they are seen by the media, national politicians, city fathers, architects, and even sometimes citizens themselves. They are seen as losing something, which must be replaced by something else through new urban techniques. I shall examine the loss of what we call in French *le lien social,* which may mean nothing else but a vague feeling of belonging, but also the bond, the unwritten contract which makes society possible.

Much more concrete is the loss of industry, and the transformation of former working-class bastions into voter reservations on the one hand, suburban office space on the other. And finally, what are the answers to such losses? At local level politicians introducing marketing techniques to better sell their city; at the level of the central state, the socialists introducing decentralisation.

Segregated urban areas

Cities in France are seen as increasingly fragmented, segregated by class and race. The main division is between centre, generally affluent, and *banlieues* (workers' flats), impoverished and sometimes sinking into despair. The paradox is that the relative efficiency of networks, especially the new métros designed to increase mobility of the working class, now increases that of the unemployed and of the underclass. It is now possible for gangs of youngsters from the *banlieues* to easily invade downtown, then riot and loot the luxury shops, of whose existence they know through another network, television.

There are rich *banlieues* where the inhabitants have chosen to live of course, but *banlieue* and *béton* (concrete) have become code words for places to which

Workers' flats east of Paris, 1993: architects Treuttel Garcias Treuttel

you're relegated. So our ghettoes are suburban, the end product of the mindless functionalism of the Charter of Athens, put into practice from the late 1950s to the 1970s in the notorious *grands ensembles*, mammoth estates of hundreds of flats, or cells.

The myth underlying the thinking of Le Corbusier and his colleagues was that of zoning: by carefully re-ordering the city, by separating its functions, it would be possible to solve social ills. We now see that the modern design of cities has increased their problems. The concentration of leisure activities in pedestrian areas for instance makes crowd-control more problematic.

Obviously the responsibility of segregation and open hostility between classes does not entirely lie with architecture and urban design. But part of the solution is seen to be architectural. Architect Roland Castro managed to convince Mitterrand in the early 1980s of the necessity of redesigning the estates in *banlieues,* and pouring billions of francs into them. It was done through *Banlieues 89,* a loose organisation of leftish architects and social workers. Its very name meant that the (then) socialist state should subsidise workers' flats again, 15 years after construction, to celebrate the values of the French revolution (89) and avoid urban violence on a large scale.

Is reintegration still possible?
The programme did achieve some results, destroying some of the worst slabs, landscaping estates, reintroducing a plurality of functions. But critics of Castro contend that *Banlieues 89* was purely cosmetic, aimed at defusing the urban crisis, or corrupting the poor, quick to understand that a good riot now and then could mean more welfare. *Banlieues 89* all but disappeared in the last years of the socialist government, but the current government seems to carry on the same policy of reintegration of estates in the city, of the poor in the body politic.

The question is, is it still possible? The erosion of the French industrial base is such that in the Red Belt around Paris (old industrial towns dominated by the communists for two or three generations) it has led to the creation of a dual society: unemployed local blue collar workers, employed white collar commuters. The architectural transcription is the bland office block next to the neo-brutalist housing estate. Industry around Paris has shed half of its labour force in the last ten years, thus destroying the close link between dark satanic mills and Red town halls.

Until then the absence of a local bourgeoisie was offset by the thousands of jobs and huge local taxes generated by industry. As factories close, or relocate to the provinces and abroad, housing estates of generally good quality are left behind. The same number of working class homes corresponds to fewer and fewer blue collar jobs, and left-wing politicians become the victims of a new form of zoning they had not anticipated.

To remain in office they have to keep their hold on their constituents, that is, continue to 'serve their needs' with supplementary benefits, good homes and good schools, stadiums, playgrounds, and even the avant-garde theatre which attracts mostly the middle-class from the other side of the ringroad. And to finance those services they are tempted to attract service industries, banks, insurance companies, which they hope will revive their tax base.

Thousands of white collar jobs are thus created in view of, but without communication with, thousands of workers' flats increasingly inhabited by unemployed Communist voters. And since the Red Town Hall will not accept detached or semi-detached houses on its turf for fear of losing political control, white collar workers are compelled to commute to even more distant, but more bourgeois *banlieues*. Needless to say, right-wing town halls similarly exclude possible left-wing voters by refusing to allow housing estates on their territories.

It is also difficult to understand the design, or absence of design, of French cities in the last decade without reference to the act of decentralisation passed in 1982. It can be summarised as follows: the central state transfers new powers and financial resources to *conseils généraux* of the 90 *départements* inherited from the French Revolution, and to 22 *conseils régionaux* created for the occasion. This increase in local power mostly applies in the fields of welfare, building and education.

Decided at the top, decentralisation was well-received by local politicians. The old Jacobin state-machine, symbolised by the *préfet*, adapted without excessive resistance, and the new decision-making bodies represented by the mayors took up their new tasks with enthusiasm. The reform has undoubtedly had the effect of an administrative shock treatment. It has led to the advent of mayor-managers, urban marketing, and the extension of the star-system to town planning and architecture.

But decentralisation has also enabled the central state to shirk its past responsibilities, and partly to wash its hands of the economic crisis and of the crisis of the welfare system. It has replaced a distant, but on the whole neutral bureaucracy with thousands of little despots motivated by precise interests. It has favoured suspicious, or even Mafia-like methods of management. The corruption which has emerged is the result above all of the logic of competition inherent in the notion of decentralisation.

The power of the mayor manager

Decentralisation has created a new type of local manager, generally a mayor-MP, or mayor-senator, the driving force behind urban and architectural projects in his constituency. It has also created a new bureaucracy, working in the fields of economics (distributing tax breaks to companies ready to threaten employment cutbacks), sports (backing for local teams, without clear democratic control), culture (inflation of schools and museums), and what the French call communication (urban marketing). Although the attempt to transform the city into merchandise, or a machine for the production of growth, has not always been so successful, there is little doubt that decentralisation has contributed to reorganise urban design in the country around two poles: economic and media-oriented, instead of the symbolic representation of the city, still in effect during the interwar period.

The symbolic role of architecture remains much more evident in Paris, where there is a duality between the 'white' city hall and the 'pink' president: the huge commissions of Mitterrand and the architectural counter-offensive of Chirac have more to do with culture and consensus in the making than with pure business.

The personalisation of public building in Paris has provided the provinces with a caricature model for the various mayors, presidents of general and regional councils. It is no longer possible to imagine a communications campaign that doesn't turn into publicity for the local despot, nor an architectural 'style' which does not become an extension of his ego, nor a worksite hoarding in which his name does not appear in block letters larger than the name of the architect.

Personalised decentralisation is no less dangerous than personal power in Paris. The mayor-MP can throw his city into debt for a century without any (public) complaint, before he's convicted of abusing social resources; he can demolish at will any local heritage; or he can oppose, at the opposite extreme, nostalgic conservation. He can finally, and this is the most frequent case, encourage a grandiloquent 'Modernism', clumsily inspired by the icons divulged by Paris, or by the new vernacular of office buildings.

French cities are changing indeed. But are they changing for the better?

The night image of the city

Ervin Y Galantay SWITZERLAND

Ervin Y Galantay is Professor of Urban Design at the Swiss Federal Technical University EPFL as well as a practising architect and planner. He has acted as a consultant to major projects in Venezuela, Nigeria, South Africa, Japan and the USA, and has completed a number of major buildings including the Library and Arts Centre at the State University of New York. His publications include *New Towns: Antiquity to Present* (1975), *New Towns in National Development* and *The Metropolis in Transition* (1985).

Architects and planners pay too much attention to the daytime city and neglect its night-image. But improving the night-image of a city is an economical way to enhance its cultural standing. Our design schools should train a new generation of designers in 'urban scenography' to take on this important role.

The image of a city is formed by perceptual experiences stored in memory. The 'readability' of the image helps orientation: the quality of the image provides 'identity' and establishes the city's attractiveness. Identification with the 'image' influences 'civic-mindedness', productivity, creativity and should be the concern of all inhabitants. As with any other phenomenon, the 'image' can be controlled and improved by a strategy for urban scenography. But who is in charge?

The logical answer would be the planners and the architects, of course. But however different these groups of professionals are, urban scenography does not seem to be their main concern. The planners – as scientists – cherish a statistical or stochastic view of the city and are concerned with the efficiency of the urban *system*. The architects – who pride themselves on being artists – are mesmerised with static *objects* and the geometrical relations of voids and volumes; they rarely consider the city as it is perceived by the individual user or actor, Much of this dichotomy is scale-related and can be traced to the rise of the modern metropolis, or even further back to the demise of the synoptic medieval world-view of the Unity of the Arts and the Sciences. One might recall the famous 1490 Milan Cathedral debate where the French architect Jean Mignot tried to argue that *'Scientia Sine Artem Nihil Est'*, but was forced to admit that the opposite is equally true *'Arts Sine Scientiam Nihil Est'*. Yet, the debate itself signalled that a cleavage had occurred.

The late Lord C P Snow in his 'Read Lectures' on the 'Two Cultures' pointed up this dichotomy which makes artists and scientists use different, mutually incomprehensible vocabularies. Lord Snow posited this theory based on his observations. He could not know the factual basis of the dichotomy which can be traced to brain-function. Since his time, the Nobel Laureates F Sperry and Sir John Eccles proved that artists and scientists perceive the world differently because of 'brain laterality': they demonstrated that the dominant left-lobe is the seat of mathematical and language skills; the right-lobe is the centre of non-verbal skills (specifically the spatial, tactile and musical abilities) and is the source of what can be called instinct or intuition.

By heredity – transmitted by the DNA molecules – people are programmed to make preferential use of either their right – or left – hemisphere. Heredity will influence their choice of profession, and specialised education will further enlarge the gap that separates the thinking processes of the artists from those of the scientists – and of the architects from those of the city planners.

Of course no one – except people with brain injuries – is exclusively dependent on either the right or the left lobe of their brain, just as no one is entirely male – or female in terms of psychological personality. These are two different but complementary sensitivities which are mutually supportive in most people, but much less well balanced in the case of highly-trained specialists.

My point is that in the case of planners and architects, both heredity and education conspired to push them in opposite directions of perception leaving a large 'no man's land' in the realm of urban scenography not sufficiently covered by either group of professionals.

Many faces of the city

A city has many faces: everyday, weekend, seasonal, festive. But even the everyday perception of the city provides us with three different readings. In the morning the city is waking up: garbage-trucks, sweepers, delivery vans, jack-hammers ripping up the tarmac, queues at bus-stops, bumper-to bumper traffic; harassed commuters. By midday people are streaming out of their work-places for lunch or for shopping; smartly dressed pedestrians are walking and enjoying the city, profiting from unplanned, random encounters. At night-time the city is one of lights with ugliness erased and key landmarks emphasised. The contrast of light and dark makes the city seductive, unpredictable, mysterious.

Planners and architects pay too much attention to the daytime city: the efficient city, the provider of goods and services, of exchange and information and of transactions. They neglect the night-time city which provides much of the magic needed to sublimate humdrum existence. At night the functional city is experienced as a stage set for pleasure, love and intrigue where everyone can be actor or spectator in reversible roles. Studies demonstrate that the best-loved cities are those whose urban scenography is conducive to spontaneous contact and para-theatrical interface. Many of these characteristics are linked to the night-image of the city.

Historical evolutions of the night image

Before the invention of gas-lighting and electricity, the night-image of our cities was dismal, gloomy and menacing – except on festive occasions, or in the case of fire or siege-warfare. Although some fixed lights might have lit up temples and palaces, the city was dark except for the moving processions of the bearers of torches and lanterns as they snaked through the narrow streets.

The most memorable night-images of a city were provided by fires caused by arson, accident or warfare. The spectacle of a siege became enhanced by the use of gunpowder and the smoke created by firearms. In the absence of war, night-time entertainment was limited to public executions which required lighting on the stage; and the burning of heretics which became the most popular night-time happening in the sixteenth century. *Auto da Fé's* peaked in Spain when the architect Juan de Herrera was ordered to design the new Plaza Mayor of Madrid to display two pyres and sufficient window-space in the surrounding facades to accommodate 30,000 spectators.

In the eighteenth century the popularity of the *Auto da Fé's* became superceded by the art of fireworks imported from China. However, the real breakthrough in terms of the night-image had to wait until the nineteenth century and the introduction of gas-lighting. Gas lanterns clearly marked the hierarchy of well-lit public buildings and main thoroughfares in contrast to the less well-lit side streets and dark alleys. To this achievement Victorian England added the new experience of the 'transparency' of buildings. The interior of a medieval cathedral may appear transparent with sunshine falling in from the outside, but seen from the exterior even heavily glazed buildings appeared opaque.

However with powerful lights installed within, the buildings revealed their interior at night-time, like the London Crystal Palace inaugurated in 1851. This architectural interest in 'revealing the innards' paralleled the scientific curiosity of seeing through the skin, leading to Röntgen's discovery of X-rays in 1890. By the *fin de siècle,* Paris acquired the reputation of the *ville lumière* with its Opera House and theatres; the glass facades of its railway stations and the innumerable candelabra for gas-lights installed along its bridges and boulevards.

The twentieth century added a few more improvements: the floodlighting of public buildings was introduced by architect Albreht Speer by using military searchlights to light up the German Pavillon at the 1937 Paris Expo. Speer must be also credited with the invention of what is today called a *Son et Lumière* show by his 1937 setting for the Nurenberg Rally and the stage-set of the tribunes where he used 150 large military searchlights vertically, to create a 'Cathedral of Light'. This spectacle so overwhelmed the British Ambassador Sir Neville Henderson that he admitted to a 'near-religious experience'. Since then, the use of spotlights on historic monuments has become general practice.

A new aspect of the night-time image of cities emerged in the twentieth century with the discovery of the 'fourth facade' of our cities; namely the vertical view from airplanes. It is well-known that the geographer Professor Jean Gottman of Oxford University discovered the phenomenon of the US Atlantic Seaboard Metropolis or 'Boswash' by taking a night-time flight from Boston to Washington. He noted that the lights formed a continuous band on the geographic scale and the fact that the structure of the megalopolis with its sinews and subcenters was clearly legible – much more so than in daytime. In fact there is the string of headlights along the motorways; the intense green-light of the interchanges: the multicolour honky-tonk of the commercial strips;

the spaced-out white lighting of the suburbs; the floodlit shopping centres and the core city areas with their transparent skyscrapers and the moving lights of advertisements at entertainment nodes like New York's Time Square.

To round up this historical survey we must add the discovery of laser technology during the last quarter of this century, used to establish a linear relation between two landmark buildings; or to enhance architectural detail; or to recreate the process of the rise of a building entity.

A tale of two European cities

Let me now tell you a 'tale of two cities' in design terms, comparing Budapest, capital of Hungary, with Bucharest, capital of Romania. In Budapest the authorities have long pursued the policy of careful conservation of all monuments and historic areas. By contrast, in Bucharest, the Stalinist dictator Ceaucescu decided to 'modernise' his capital with one stroke, by demolishing the historical core area of Bucharest to create vast avenues flanked by prefabricated blocks of flats and public buildings. This cultural lobotomy was accompanied by the destruction of hundreds of villages considered to be sub-economic in terms of scale and with the goal of driving the rural inhabitants to larger towns to provide workers in megalomaniac industrial projects.

All this misguided investment ran up the national debt so Ceaucescu – in order to reduce the foreign indebtedness – launched an energy-saving policy by restricting the use of household electricity to a single 40 watt light bulb per dwelling unit, and strictly enforced this rule by his police, supported by a network of informers. With this, Ceaucescu turned Bucharest into a city of darkness and gloom, where a posting as an ambassador came to be considered as a punitive assignment.

Meanwhile Budapest pursued the opposite policy; the city fathers insisted on flooding Budapest in light and projected the image of a 'City of Lights', of enlightenment and of opening to the world. Prophets of doom raised their voices against the light shows: 'How can we afford this...? the money would be better spent elsewhere... ridiculous ostentation, etc'. But floodlit Budapest boosted the Hungarian ego while the Romanians sank into ever more aggressive Dracula-type gloom.

This contrast was not lost on visitors. Budapest is rated among the hottest destinations for tourism and as a venue for congresses. Since 1989 Hungary has attracted more Western investment than all other Eastern European countries combined. As more transparent office buildings and advertising signs are added to the night image, the city is ever more radiating an exuberant *joie de vivre*.

Now I don't want to claim that light-effects alone are responsible for the economic revival of Budapest, but the psychological impact helps to sell an image and also raises the pride and civic mindedness of the inhabitants. As a result Budapest is also a notably cleaner city than Bucharest, and there is less vandalism than elsewhere.

Training of an urban scenographer

At present there is hardly any instruction in how to master the use of artificial light in design schools in Europe. Future urban scenographers need instruction in urban history, stage design, lighting, urban scenography, large-scale model-building and computer simulation techniques. Once trained, the urban scenographer could work as a freelance consultant, but could also be attached to a city-planning commission with a special brief of caring for the city's image and especially its night-image.

Medieval Italian cities used to have municipal officers named *Sopraintendonte della Ornata* – with a special responsibility to dress up the city for special festivities and to cultivate a dignified image fostering the city's cultural identity. Similarly, the urban scenographers could be made responsible for all ephemeral aspects of artistic enrichment of public space. For example they could designate bare party-walls around building-sites and parking lots as 'graffiti opportunities' or assign these surfaces to artists to be covered with murals and *trompe l'oeil* paintings. Urban scenographers should also provide ideas for such mobile 'decor carriers' as trolleys, tramways, buses and riverboats. Above all, the urban scenographer should be in charge of the night image and this should be thought of as an educational instrument helping orientation and the understanding of the urban structure, but also a source of visual entertainment. Being neither a scientist nor an artist – not a planner nor an architect – the urban scenographer should aspire, above all, to become a successful *magician*.

Investment in managing the night image of the city can bring economic and cultural benefits

Restaurant stairs at Hotel Otaru Marittimo, Japan, 1989: Branson
Coates Architecture

The Japanese context: manipulator or manipulated?

Sy Chen JAPAN

Born in Beijing, **Sy Chen** founded Creative Intelligence Associates in 1986. The consultancy, a consortium of architects, interior designers, artists and operation specialists from around the globe, coined the widely used media term 'space production'. Sy Chen has worked on a range of projects including the Penrose Institute Museum, the Architect Building in New York, and the Wild Blue Yokohama surfing pool, collaborating with architects including Joseph Lembo and Nigel Coates.

The media-fanned introduction of celebrity architecture into Japan in the late 1980s reflected the transient demands of an overheated economy hungry for European style. It also introduced the 'architectural producer' – an impresario of the built environment, whose approach has survived the bursting of the media bubble.

Japan underwent drastic changes in the post-war period. The economy expanded at double-digit rates in the 1950s through to the mid-1970s. Growth in the latter half of the 1970s slowed to about 5 per cent, then averaged 4 per cent in the 1980s. While the economy attained respectable growth in the 1980s by world standards, it is experiencing more moderate expansion in the 1990s. The dramatic rise of the yen from the middle of the 1980s opened Japan to western financiers and interests, and vastly increased Japan's capacity to buy imports. Movement of people to and from Japan also increased, with the number of foreign visitors rising about half as fast as the number of Japanese who went overseas. The yen's renewed rise in 1993 will further boost this revolution in international contact.[1]

Many now see Japan's surge in the late 1980s as an aberration, however, fuelled by cheap credit and the unprecedented boom in land and stock values. Unbridled speculation and greed, and a preoccupation with materialism, eventually led to the collapse of the overheated bubble economy. The free-wheeling 1980s blinkered many Japanese from the reality that the economy had been on a go-slow trend for years. But for all its shortcomings this temporary blind-spot brought what seemed like limitless opportunities for architects and designers to be involved in a wide range of projects. It was a time when the Japanese eagerly consumed 'designer' buildings, just as they purchased sharp, fashionable apparel, unconventional holiday destinations and personal 'lifestyles'.

Technology, media and communications

Japan in the late 1980s was a country operating on a seemingly never-ending extended play, accelerated by the speed of information production, transmission and 'downloading'. This mindset in turn stimulated appetites for instant consumption. Unlike many countries in Europe and North America, Japan appears to have distinct channels of media communication and processing. The media operates through a complex filtering system. Raw, unadulterated information from abroad goes through absorbing layers and filters in Tokyo. Each stage sifts out what is pure while introducing biases and skewed interpretations from various commercial interests. This processed information is then passed on to regional centres throughout the Japanese archipelago, where it undergoes further stages of sifting and reinterpretation. Messages often undergo more transformations than fiction, because of the role assigned to news and information by contemporary social and political institutions.[2]

Misinterpretation of the original information and its meaning may occur, but if things are progressing smoothly, people cease to become conscious of any problem with it. Context is vital to interpretation, and this is especially so in a post-Babel world in which people do not speak with one tongue. They will cease to worry about the purity of the information source as soon as they become preoccupied with new information.

In the late 1980s, the Japanese openly thrived upon an information overload. They actually enjoyed being inundated by it. They didn't want to think about how information and technology become a dominating force that challenges basic cultural and societal value systems. Instead, they enjoyed choosing from a seemingly endless number of options and selections.

If a designer understood the way this system worked, it was almost child's play to manipulate and to bring the media to bear upon a particular strategy or purpose. Over-exposure of the designer, or instant celebrity, prompted the media to devour or manipulate that celebrity for purposes totally unintended and sometimes unwanted by the designer. A full understanding of the control media and technology exert and how they create their own organisational structures, ethics and values became an essential for all designers. I took a very cautious approach to promoting my projects, and the designers and architects in our consortium, through the Japanese media. I think I avoided the pitfalls experienced by many others who failed to develop effective tactics of resistance.

In Japan, it is very important to maintain a global viewpoint when presenting your thoughts to the media. Global means more than international. Global means more than multicultural. Global means envisioning a world free of national borders. This is a world where the burgeoning flow of information directly to consumers and individuals gives them the freedom and the desire to make their own choices. Here it is possible for the many variations in taste around the world to find concrete expression.[3] Failure to project this understanding when confronting the Japanese media in particular for amateurish handling of social, economic, ideological, political and cultural implications of mass media in general, may mean you are treated as a mere phenomenon, an oddity, a curio.

The alternative CIA

I am known as an 'architectural producer' or 'space producer', the 'driving force' who breathes life and energy into an architectural design project. This description of the profession is perhaps unique to Japan. Invariably, clients come to me when they find the project under development beyond the capacity or capability of any ordinary architect or designer. Often clients find themselves in need of a highly creative architect or designer who can adapt to problematic project environments. This demands strong concepts which will differentiate the project from the rest. It also requires operational specialists who are able to realise the long-term programme and an agent to ensure returns on the investment projections. We often find projects are a combination of any number of these activities.

Like a motion picture director, I envisage a scenario in my mind and cast a global production team from our consortium of architects, art directors, interior designers, illustrators, restaurateurs, hotel owners, museum directors, and entertainment and amusement park specialists. The consortium is called Creative Intelligence Associates. It is the alternative CIA.

CIA and Nigel Coates

The success of the Metropole project in Tokyo, my first with the English architect Nigel Coates, was a turning point. The Metropole was an oriental restaurant with a library cafe. This project was largely reminiscent of my successful undertaking in Hollywood, the China Club, in 1980. It led me to establish CIA, a platform to introduce young and creative architects from different countries around the world in Japan through new and exciting projects. As an 'architectural producer', prospective investors gave me the freedom to suggest and realise new concepts. It was a challenge to form a production team of different artists and craftsmen from Britain, and transport them to Tokyo to add narrative layers of architecture.

In fact it was my first meeting with Nigel Coates in London in 1985 that inspired me to realise his narrative architecture in Tokyo. At that time Tokyo favoured the minimalist and functional direction represented in Tadao Ando's buildings. I saw in Nigel's work a materialisation of the territory of ideas. This was environmental design equated with the theatre of the sign, the unexpected pitched against the familiar, the hard against the soft, the enclosed against the fluid. Since 1986 we have undertaken many projects in Tokyo together. These have included Caffe Songo, the Takeo Kikuchi Shop and The Wall.

The Wall project in 1990 was an attempt to provide a partial solution to the accelerated speed at which people consume space in Tokyo. Our alternative was to provide a malleable shell which anticipates that, over the next 30 years, tenants will evolve and change according to their own needs.

1993 saw the first of our projects with Nigel Coates in the post-bubble period. The Penrose Institute in Tokyo is being planned with great emphasis on operations. It will be a revolutionary vertical gallery tower under the curation of London's Institute of Contemporary Art. It will encourage experimentation and innovation in all art forms, and provide a proving ground for new work and a forum for new ideas.

Global visions for the 1990s

Since its inception in the 1980s, CIA has diversified into a broad range of projects. We now collaborate with many other international architects to realise our global vision for architectural design in Japan. Our activities now incorporate the genius of designers and architects from Los Angeles, New York, Barcelona and Moscow. One of our most recent projects, a collaboration between Josh Schweitzer of Schweitzer BIM and Rick Seireeni of Studio Seireeni, Los Angeles, opened in April 1993. The Big Life, at a length of 540 meters, is the longest sports bar in the world. It boasts a 1,000-seat capacity and a daily turnover of up to 8,000 people.

Pivotal to the success of this project was making operation planning and training the top priority before initiating the design phase. Unlike many of the design-focused projects in the 1980s, the key to successful project achievement in the 1990s will largely depend upon two factors. First of all, the calibre and professionalism of the operation specialists you provide. Second, how you train them to envisage and produce the project from a total perspective, and anticipate the experience of the project when completed.

What will happen to Japan?

Over the last few years, analysts have noted that, for the first time in four centuries, the world's economic axis is shifting back to the Pacific Rim. Inter-regional trade and investment flows in the area are on the rise. There is a natural complementarity between resource-rich nations such as America, the ASEAN group, and Australia on the one hand, and resource-poor, industrial economies like Japan and ANIEs on the other. The Asia-Pacific region has a great degree of diversity in race, religion, culture, tradition and values. The various stages of social and economic development is a strength. If we respect the diversity, vitality will spring forth.[4]

Some now boldly forecast the dawning of a century dominated by a tribe of pioneering, inter-linked Chinese entrepreneurs. The Chinese-based economy that spans the mainland and a score of other countries in East Asia has resisted the global recession plaguing virtually every advanced industrial nation.[5] This notion of a Chinese commonwealth encompasses an array of political and economic systems bound together by a shared tradition, not simply by geography. It is the type of global network beginning to span all continents that many western multinationals have tried to create in their own organisations.[6]

Where does this leave Japan? One school of thought places Japan at the head of a 'flying geese formation' of East Asian nations. Japan is already the leading foreign investor in almost every regional economy. Nine out of ten of

EDDIE VALENTINE HANE

Exterior view of The Wall, Nishi Azabu, Tokyo, 1990: Branson Coates Architecture

its largest foreign aid recipients are located in East Asia. In addition, Japan exports more technology to Asia than anywhere else.

However, a retired Tokyo University professor has made a dramatic, yet bleak, forecast. Japan, he insists, might find itself merely part of a Chinese economic umbrella by the year 2015. Fully acknowledging the dynamism of Chinese enterprise, he bases his theories on Japan's inherent weaknesses when compared with the rapidly growing Asian nations: the constant shortage of labour; the lack of innovation and invention to develop new technologies; a rapidly greying population exacerbated by a low birth rate; and the lack of effective military forces.

Despite these words of caution, though, an evolution may be taking place in Japan. The break-up of the monolithic ruling party signals that the politics of Japan are changing because the people of Japan are changing. Admiration for individualism is spreading, and women are gradually challenging the traditional status of men.

Japan is searching for its direction and identity in the twenty-first century. There is a need to look for something which transcends the western view of the mind altogether. This may come through the re-evaluation of the ways of the eastern mind. Is there something in this notion of mind which improves upon a focus on thinking, intelligence and rationality in cognitive science? This would focus instead on feeling, spirit and consciousness.

Design, media and society

Japan's wealth has brought aspirations and desires corresponding to those of a bold, mature, fully participating 'nation of the world'. We are experiencing a dramatic re-structuring of every aspect of life and society in Japan. The relationship between design and media somehow suggests the way Marshall Berman defined the traditions of Modernism: 'To be modern is to find ourselves in an enviroment that provides us with adventure, power, joy, growth, transformation of ourselves and the world and, at the same time, that threatens to destroy everything we have, everything we know.'[7]

We are living in a revolutionary age, where technology and communications fragment our existence into numerous shards of disparate yet inter-related experience. We are conscious of living in multiple worlds simultaneously where disunity finds a mate in unity. We must be concerned with contributing to our world in meaningful and lasting ways. Design has an important role to play in this ethos. It can help make sense of the overwhelming babble, help us to understand the forest of symbols. To make creative contributions in a modern society endowed – or is it afflicted? – with turbo-powered information media means to make sense of the fact that, as Marx wrote, 'All that is solid melts into air'.

References

1. 'Changing Japan: The World Breaks In', *The Economist*, London, June 26, 1993, p21.
2. Casmir, Fred L, 'Mass Communication and Culture', in Korzenny, et al, *Mass Media Effects Across Cultures* (Sage Publications, Newbury Park, London, New Dehli, 1992)
3. Ohmae, Kenichi, *The Borderless World: Power and Strategy in the Interlinked Economy* (Harper Business, New York, 1990)
4. Leuenberger, Theodor and Weinstein, Martin E, Eds, *Europe, Japan and America in the 1990s: Cooperation and Competition* (Springer-Verlag, Berlin, 1992)
5. Kotkin, J, 'The Chinese Century: Are We Ready for This Powerful Global Tribe?', *The Washington Post*, Washington DC, Oct 4, 1992
6. Rao, John, 'The Worldwide Web of Chinese Business', in *Harvard Business Review*, Boston, March-April, 1993
7. Berman, Marshall, *All That is Solid Melts Into Air* (Simon and Schuster, New York, 1982)

Balancing public conscience and private initiatives

John Worthington ENGLAND

John Worthington is Director of the Institute of Advanced Architectural Studies, University of York, and Deputy Chairman of DEGW, the international firm of architects, designers and planners. He has undertaken strategic space planning consultancy for a number of multinational firms both in the UK and on the continent. He is President of the Urban Design Group and a Vice President of the Architectural Association.

Public place-making has declined in Britain as the cult of the individual has replaced community values, and the globalisation of business has devalued local city character. But the urban designer has a key role to play in setting a new agenda and establishing the vision to revitalise the public realm.

In the last 30 years in Britain, we have witnessed a continuing decline in community values, and a concern for the public realm. A recent review of the public place-making in Greater London was a catalogue of piecemeal decisions, visual anarchy and declining standards. Current attitudes to urban design are coloured by the underlying trends of a society which is moving towards: purely commercial values, and a belief that private interests and market forces will look after the environment; the 'enterprise society' in which those who help themselves will succeed; the cult of the individual, with less concern for the community; a globalisation of business, and with it a sameness of place, and a reduction of local character and values; and networked enterprises, that have learnt to work across traditional boundaries of space and time.

The Thatcher years of the 1980s saw a collapse of the welfare state, and a dismantling of strong centralist city government. Today there is little regard for the care, design and upkeep of the urban realm. London has no focus for governance; Manchester, Birmingham, Glasgow and Leeds are all struggling to sustain their civic vision. In the UK, most cities have failed to value design. They have no focused overall responsibility for urban design (Birmingham being a notable exception); and they divested themselves of responsibility for public places, through privatising functions and services.

A balanced approach

The traditional high street with its broad mix of shops and bustle has been superceded by the even quality, sanitised, high security, privatised realm of the covered shopping mall. In inner city residential areas, the 'doorstep' community spirit of the Victorian terraces has been superceded by housing estates with vandalised lift wells, and neglected patches of green.

But as the tidal wave of 1980s commercial development fades, it is being replaced by a more balanced approach. There is a search for quality of life rather than merely the materialistic pressure to increase gross national product, and a recognition of the need to manage change through consultation and participation.

Major schemes such as Coin Street, and King's Cross, which are areas of national and international significance, have highlighted the need to both listen to local neighbourhood concerns, and place these demands in a wider context. Stanhope Properties seminars on Managing Urban Change[1], which brought together community developers, financiers, users and academics, clearly showed that often both so-called 'sides' had the same objectives. Stanhope's document *Collaborative Development*[2] shows the wide range of activities caring developers can involve themselves in to create successful development where everyone wins.

Business in the Community has shown that a corporate social conscience can bring pressure to bear for economic improvement, and the most successful of the City Challenge schemes, based on public-private partnering, have identified how financial resources and human energy can be unleashed.

Perhaps the most interesting trend is a shift from a backward-looking view of conservation as preservation, to a concept of place-making, which understands the past, but develops for the future. Areas such as the Merchant City in Glasgow, Covent Garden in London and Birmingham Jewellery Quarter have built on the past to create a thriving future. Conservation studies now increasingly concern themselves with the sensitive husbanding of resources for the future, whilst respecting the heritage of the past.

Historical perspective

History allows us to reflect on very different attitudes to the public realm. The medieval city's main areas of exchange were the church, city hall and market place. There was a blurred boundary between public, institutional and private space. The Renaissance saw an increasing articulation and continuity of public space from exterior plazas to interior meeting spaces and an overlap between Church, State and Commerce.

Nolle's figure ground plan of Rome makes no distinction between internal and external public space, and provides us with a new perception of spatial sequence. Haussman's plan for Paris in the 1850s was the precursor of modern planning, with a separation of functions, definition of building lines, and a strong division between public space and private property. The Parisian Mansion Block of 1853 (Leonardo Benevelo[3]) created a clear delineation at the façade between the public realm and private property. The flats within were stratified according to position.

Modern Movement city planning, as exemplified by the zoned functions of Le Corbusier's Ville Radieuse, dismembered the integration of earlier ages. Today the public realm has become privatised, themed and sanitised. Shopping centres such as Meadowhall, Sheffield, or city-centre covered malls, are privately owned and separately policed. The new meeting spaces in today's city are frequently in the private domain, and increasingly exclusive; the hotel lobby, shopping centres, airport concourses, colleges and offices.

The historic city integrated public, institutional and private space

Healthy city structures

DEGW research in areas such as Covent Garden[4], South Shoreditch[5] and the Merchant City[6] suggests that healthy city centres are founded on:

- A vibrant mix of uses that match the varying quality and configuration of space available, and wide range of rentals achievable. The death of the city is the rental contour approach, which breeds uniformity and drives out richness and diversity.
- A synergistic network of small and large businesses, undertaking complementary and supporting functions, not single-use land zoning. The local economic network in Covent Garden, which had grown up around the Royal Opera House, graphically presented the need for mixed uses.
- A managed process of change which builds on the heritage of the past, but allows appropriate development for the future.
- A capitalisation of existing resources in terms of buildings, uses, institutions and people. So often the most-needed resource for successful urban regeneration is local commitment. But too many regeneration plans underestimate the initiatives already on the ground, however frail, and aim to reinvent the wheel.
- Community commitment which is co-ordinated and animated by strong local leadership.

Action planning

There is a well-established and growing experience in both North America and Europe of planning through participation. In North America the American Institute of Architects (AIA) Urban Design Assistance Teams (UDATs) have brilliantly set the precedent of professionals providing their time over a short, intensive period to help communities establish their goals, and prepare a vision and blueprint for the future.

In the UK, the Urban Design Group (UDG) has championed this cause, with events at Wood Green (Haringey) and Hammersmith in London. At Burgess Park in Southwark, London[8], I chaired a Business in the Community action-planning event aimed at identifying issues, setting goals, considering achievable options and proposing a vision for an unloved and unsafe park once envisaged as a 'green lung' from the Elephant and Castle to Greenwich. The event lasted two days and involved a mixed team of lawyers, accountants, surveyors, architects, landscapers and communicators. Managing change is never easy, but within a year some progress had been made.

Revitalising the public realm

If we are to reinvigorate the public realm, we must reintroduce a sense of civic interest in the role, management and quality of our centres. Urban design, as the skill of place-making through time, has all but disappeared from most city planning departments.

But the urban designer has a unique role to play in identifying issues and providing clear problem statements. The urban designer can set goals and establish a vision: Croydon's recent exhibition organised with the Architecture Foundation[9] used the design imagination of 14 practices to set an agenda for a future Croydon. Finally, the urban designer can communicate opportunities and facilitate action through time – the animateur who manages and steers all the disparate interest groups to a common vision.

References

1. Managing Urban Change, a series of four seminars organised by DEGW for Stanhope Properties.
2. *Collaborative Development,* Stanhope Properties
3. *The History of the City* by Leonardo Benevolo (Scholar Press London 1980)
4. 'Study of Covent Garden Businesses', URBED and DEGW, London, 1976.
5. Services in the City Fringe: Accommodation Requirements of Service Sector Companies in South Shoreditch. Report for Rosehaugh Stanhope Developments, DEGW, London 1986.
6. Merchant City Glasgow, a study for the Scottish Development Agency by DEGW Glasgow.
7. Urban Design in Action. Peter Batchelor and David Lewis, North Carolina State, University 1985.
8. Report of the Burgess Park Action Team, Business in the Community, London 1993.
9. 'Croydon the Future', A special supplement of *Blueprint,* London 1993.

The malling of the world

Rodney Fitch ENGLAND

Rodney Fitch is Executive Chairman of Fitch, one of the world's largest and best-known design consultancies. The practice is multi-disciplinary and active on projects throughout the world ranging from architecture, through interiors and graphic design to product development and industrial and engineering design. Fitch is a former President of the Chartered Society of Designers, a member of the British Design Council and a Trustee of the Victoria and Albert Museum.

US-style shopping malls have irrevocably altered the character of cities and communities all over the world. They are undeniably popular, but are they also an environmentally-damaging exercise in cultural imperialism? The task ahead is for mall designers to enhance rather than obliterate a local sense of place.

I do not intend this to be a polemic for or against the architectural design of the shopping malls or centres. Rather, I want look at them as an amazing feat of our times, from their origins in the potato fields of America to their development, refinement and export all over the world.

Some critics, of course, wish this process had never happened. They would have the rest of the world left bare of shopping centres, arguing that such a culturally imperialist phenomenon – taking Ohio to Jakarta – threatens to destroy local cultural identity. They fret that these new developments change the dynamics of local life by sucking the centre out of cities, by creating environmental blight and job losses. Environmentalists protest at the spoilation of the countryside to create green field sites, and the growth of business and traffic in outlying areas.

Some of this, of course, is true, but consumers, not surprisingly, rather like the idea of shopping centres. These cathedrals of the modern age have sometimes approached an artform in recent years in terms of refinement, sophistication and fantasy play. I have been to shopping centres in Louisville, Texas, where the retail architecture is inspired by the great pyramids, summoning visitors not to burial grounds but to shop until you drop, and to Georgetown, Washington DC, where the architects and designers have tried to evoke an atmosphere of the past so that shoppers imagine they might bump into Mark Twain or George Washington whilst shopping for Armani or Vuitton.

And far from destroying the urban fabric, some shopping and leisure malls have provided a focus for regeneration. The Magna Plaza shopping centre in the centre of Amsterdam, an old post office building of great merit rescued from the scrapheap of history and recycled with verve, and the Mediterranean-inspired Pavilions shopping centre in Uxbridge, west London, which restores a heart to a place destroyed by the sterile and soulless Modernist architecture of the seventies, are examples from my own practice which demonstrate this point. Or I could point to the imaginative retail regeneration of St Louis railway station by HOK, or to the regeneration of Baltimore and a whole string of locations by the Rouse Group. Such is the popular appeal that one is left to ask that if shopping and leisure malls didn't exist in the 1990s, wouldn't we have to invent them for the end of the twentieth century?

A sense of community

This Design Renaissance congress began by exploring the notion, in the words of the British designer Michael Wolff, of a 'we-feeling' which the design profession has a duty to communicate and enhance. If malls do provide a 'we-feeling', as many people suggest they do, then is it because they provide the physical cornerstone of a community – safe, secure, weatherproofed, convenient, stimulating and comfortable – and with it, a sense of community and community pride? Or are the critics really right in claiming that the mall building destroys the way of life for indigenous populations?

In this context I am reminded of a story told by the English author, researcher and 'urban anthropologist' Peter York. His partner went to a Stockholm environment conference in the early 1970s and sat through session after session in which people complained that the world was getting worse, pollution was mounting, fish were dying, and stuff like that. Eventually some nameless, brave Third World delegate stood up and said: 'Let us in the starving Third World have some of your pollution please, and everything else that goes with it!' York's point is that while it is easy to poke fun at or disapprove of the culture of the US shopping mall when you have access and can take or leave it, those without access can only stand in wonder and are not remotely jaded by what they behold.

All malled out?

Nevertheless it must be said that while much of the world has taken enthusiastically to the idea of the US shopping mall, American consumers are less enthusiastic about the 'mall experience' after the indulgences of the 1980s and are visiting them less often. According to Jeanne Giordiano, an American urban planner who has worked on the Grand Central Terminal development in New York, the biggest growth in shopping malls took place between 1970 and 1985 by which time there were no suburbs without a shopping mall and no downtown without a festival market development either completed or on the books. But in the late 1980s, the large department stores, which had been the anchors and the bloodline of these malls, got caught up in leveraged buyouts and started to disappear. The stock market crash of 1987, which swallowed up some developers, didn't help either. No anchors, no malls. But equally the new US phenomenon of the warehouse club – huge, democratic and astoundingly cheap – has begun to wean the US customer away from malls.

My own observations chime with those of Jeanne Giordiano: that retail in America today is in flux and that people have more places to shop than they could possibly use. There is, it is claimed, a shopping centre every five miles or so. In

1964 every man, woman and child in the US had about 5 sq ft of retail space to himself or herself. As of 1990, they have about 18 sq ft, and as Peter York points out, had it not been for the recession they would have had 20 sq ft. In the UK, there is 12 sq ft of retail space per head of population, which is still good going compared to the Pacific Rim countries where the race is on to catch up on the western-style shopping environment and ethic. In Indonesia, the Philippines and in Singapore, huge shopping developments – some of 5 million sq ft – are being built. But staggering as this will be to some and sad to others, remember some 10 per cent of the world's population live in the Pacific Rim and Jakarta alone has a population of some eight million souls.

Back in America, the birthplace of the mall, the genre is now in the process of reinventing itself. There are new anchors to hook shoppers. To the ubiquitous food courts, we now welcome everything from casinos to fantasy theme parks. The stakes have also been raised by the development of a new form of shopping centre, far larger than anything we have seen before.

The Mall of America

The Mall of America at Bloomington, Minneapolis, or Mega-Mall as it is colloquially called, was built as a supreme act of faith against a background of deep recession and gloom. As such, it wins an Oscar as the anti-trend development of the decade. Conventional retail wisdom has it that large-scale shopping malls are dead ducks, that the new centres of the 90s must be smaller, more convenient, more specialised. The Mall of America is more than big: constructed at a cost of £500 million, it covers 4.25 million sq ft of space (of which 2.6 million sq ft is retail space), and has more than 300 shops, four anchor department stores (Bloomingdales, Macy's, Nordstrom and Sears), and a cast of thousands. It was conceived not as an isolated shopping mall but as a small city.

At the centre of the project, a seven-acre Camp Snoopy indoor theme part has 23 different rides and dozens of other attractions. There are also cinemas, nightclubs, theatres and bars. A second phase is planned which will add an aquarium, hotel and more retail, pushing the total size to around 5.5 million sq ft at a cost of £700 million. At any one time there might be 10,000 people in the complex. One day 200,000 people visited the centre. Its strong emotional appeal comes in part from its successful integration of many typical city activities – shopping, leisure, learning, entertainment – within the mall environment. As well as many interesting shops, the centre also boasts some good services. It will rent you a mobile phone or a pager or a small electric cart if you don't want to walk through the different sunlit 'neighbourhoods' of the mall.

I am enthusiastic about the Mall of America for a number of reasons: its bucking of a trend on a giant scale with the creation of a self-contained city; its spirit of optimism reflected in such a colossal investment in a period of recession; its distinctive relation between shopping and leisure, a relationship in which the edges are *not* blurred; and the way good design has contributed mightily to the project in making such a large space efficient and appealing.

In my view, the design element of the Mall of America reflects two of the overriding arguments for the use of design in retail environments. The first is political: design makes manifest a customer's right to choice and is therefore an essential aspect of any functioning democracy. It is through design that people express their desire for change, their desire for better artefacts and experiences that add quality to their lives. Design prospers in democratic societies. In command economies, there is little in the way of design – or consumer choice. To opt for design is to express a definite and optimistic choice about the future.

Remember that it is one of the more ironic footnotes of history that Gorbachev once admitted to a reporter that he realised the Soviet collectivist cause was doomed and that the process of *perostroika* should be speeded up following his visit to see the vast array of goods in the giant Marks & Spencer store at Marble Arch in London in the mid-80s.

The second argument for design is the emotional argument. It is perhaps the more powerful because it involves a direct appeal to people's senses. Shopping should be a tactile and sensory experience. The attitudes and responses of consumers are conditioned by their senses and emotions. Design can appeal to them because people can touch, see, smell and hear design.

Resonances of proportion, scale and composition; the revelation of vistas and visual images; sounds and smells coming from a bakery or pasta store ... these are the sensory qualities that influence hearts as well as minds. And they are evident in the design of the Mall of America. Good design speaks to the inner person – to the designer or the design critic that is within everyone. It is a way of communicating. It speaks a universal language that needs no translation; it crosses national and cultural barriers, and of course it has been seen to be effective in a global trading context which is why designers and architects have played such a prominent role in the malling of the world.

Economic and cultural fragility

But for all the optimism engendered by the Mall of America, I am aware that this global process of malling carries with it a host of concerns. As each new development goes up, what will its impact be on fragile adjacent urban economies? And, looking further down the line, what will be the impact of low-cost discount shopping and computer-driven teleshopping on the malls? Could they become irrelevant and abandoned, just like we abandoned our old factories and dockland warehouses?

The cry inevitably goes up that we need more planning restrictions to stop these alienating blots on the landscape, these anonymous, lookalike products of US cultural imperialism. I must say immediately that I am a free marketeer. I am against the restrictions of the nanny state, and its plethora of planning laws which tell us what we can and cannot do. However I am also very concerned about preserving the cultural heritage of nations, their cities and their landscapes – always provided that the people's choice is paramount.

In Europe, which has plainly taken to the US mall concept, there are examples which show that it is possible to have extensive shopping centre

Entrance to the Mall of America, Bloomington, Minneapolis (top).
This mega-mall incorporates a seven-acre Camp Snoopy indoor theme
park (below)

development which retains an element of national character. There are a number of good centres: Richard Rogers even built a staggeringly interesting development in France. Equally, there are many bad examples in Europe which deny any sense of cultural history or identity, and whose bad example the Third World would certainly not want to follow.

Take Glasgow, the city of Design Renaissance. It has two shopping centres. One is an example of spaceship glass-box venacular parachuted into Scotland from Houston or Dallas or wherever without any reference to context. I am affronted that such a development was allowed to take place in a city of Glasgow's rich heritage. The other is a shopping centre I greatly admire: Princes Square is at the other end of the scale, an exquisite refurbishment which draws its inspiration from turn-of-the-century Glasgow history, and the interrelationship of Art Nouveau with the Vienna Secession. Here is an example which any city, proud of its architectural heritage but determined to give its citizens choice and quality, would be glad to provide.

The tale of these two shopping centres in Glasgow demonstrates that the bottom line on this issue can often come down to a question of the responsibilities and actions of the designer. The malling of the world will continue because people want malls and people enjoy them. It is up to the designers and architects who work on such projects to show sensitivity, skill, imagination and courage – and produce some evidence in their work that they understand the cultural nuances of the cities and communities which will be affected by these developments.

Princes Square shopping centre, Glasgow: sensitive to city's rich architectural heritage

A renaissance for Glasgow

Stuart Gulliver SCOTLAND

Stuart Gulliver has been Chief Executive of the Glasgow Development Agency since 1991. He was previously Regional Director of the Scottish Development Agency and has also worked with Warrington New Town Development Corporation. Gulliver is a Visiting Professor in Economic and Social Research at Glasgow University.

Glasgow, the city which hosted the Design Renaissance congress, is itself planning a renaissance. An ambitious post-industrial strategy is being implemented by the Glasgow Development Agency to make the city more commercially and culturally competitive in Europe by the year 2000.

This paper is about the way Glasgow is setting about the task of quite deliberately reinventing itself to create a future for the city. A great deal has happened in Glasgow since the late 1970s and early 1980s, but the pace and scale of change needs to be even greater in the 1990s if the city is to compete more effectively.

The Glasgow Development Agency (GDA), formed in April 1991, is the lead economic development organisation in the city. It has a budget of £72 million and employs 155 people. Its activities embrace property, business and environmental development, training and marketing. In developing a business plan for the GDA, we took the opportunity to stand back a little and look at the city *as a whole*. Rather than identify individual projects and aggregate them, we took a top-down approach – a view of the city from 10 miles up. We looked at the city rather like a private company – and asked the kind of questions you would ask of a company.

Who are Glasgow's competitive cities and what are they up to? What are Glasgow's strengths and weaknesses, opportunities and threats? How is Glasgow performing as a city? How will it perform over the next 10 to 15 years? Where does Glasgow want to be? What is amenable to change – and what is not? This analogy of the city with the private company is useful in thinking about the future, but there are limits to it. I'll mention just two. Firstly, in a private company there is little doubt about what constitutes that company. But what actually is a city? In Glasgow, seven local authorities make up what I would call the 'sphere of influence' of the city – in terms of the labour market, housing market, and journeys to work. But although the City of Glasgow has a population of some 700,000, metropolitan Glasgow has about 1.5 million people. Timescale is a second distinguishing factor. The process of transforming a city takes at least a generation – 25 years – whereas it is possible to turn a company round in three to five years. Therefore deliberate thought needs to be given to managing the process of change in a city – with deliberate markers, pacing devices if you like, every two or three years to signify that the direction of change is along the right lines.

Competitive analysis of cities

We made a competitive analysis of the performance of *non-capital cities* in Europe with a population in the order of one million, in the context of three forms of prosperity: *business prosperity* (economic performance, wealth generation, growth rates, new firm formation, gross national product per head); *people prosperity* (economic welfare, standard of living, levels of income, skill, education and unemployment); and *place prosperity* ('livability' and urban quality).

What did this analysis show? We contrived this analysis into a football league system. Division 1: Milan, Hamburg, Amsterdam, Barcelona. Division 2: Lyon, Marseille, Turin, Antwerp. Division 3: Naples, Birmingham, Glasgow, Manchester. Division 4: Bremen, Lille, Valencia, Essen. Glasgow is in the Third Division along with other British cities. However, if this analysis had been done in 1980, Glasgow would probably have been a non-league club.

As a result of this competitive analysis, Glasgow has set itself the following target over the next 10 years. Glasgow's aim is to reposition itself at the top of Division 2 by the turn of the century and is putting in place developments, activities and programmes to achieve that position. If it is to move from a traditional to an advanced industrial city, then Glasgow needs a kick-start and major impetus to narrow the gap in the next decade.

The past ten years in Glasgow

What has happened to Glasgow over the past decade? There are many ways of describing the change but let us consider it under five headings. First, it has been needs-driven in working to repair the damage – a series of initiatives have tracked the effects of urban decline in both inner and outer areas of the city. Second, it has been opportunity-driven in seeking to exploit its best features with urban core revitalisation, support for indigenous companies, urban beautification and enhancement, and inward investment. Third, it has developed new urban products including the Scottish Exhibition and Conference Centre, Burrell Gallery, International Concert Hall, McLellan Galleries, major retailing developments, and the expansion of Glasgow International Airport.

Fourth, it has introduced new urban processes such as the Glasgow's Miles Better Campaign and Glasgow Action (a private-public partnership body). Finally, Glasgow has been image-driven in developing head-turning events such as the Glasgow Garden Festival in 1988 (4.5 million visitors in six months) and the European City of Culture programme in 1990. These are what could be described as pacing devices.

Developing a new approach

What, then, is required in the 1990s to close the gap and accelerate change? First of all, what is needed is a city-wide view. The city needs to be tackled as a whole – over an appropriate market area. Such a view of the city would embrace not only the central urban area but adjacent suburbs and settlements. This realistic view of economic space reflects more accurately how the city economy actually operates. Policy and strategy should be directed across the economic sphere of influence of the city rather than particular territorial segments such as the inner-city. It is the competitiveness of the whole that is of paramount concern: in effect, the 'city as project'.

Secondly, we need to create a shared vision for the whole city. Confidence is needed to turn any city around and a formal pre-requisite of confidence is a far-sighted and inspirational vision of what the city should be, what it can be, and an ability to communicate that vision to everyone. This vision must be shared by local authorities, private sector, development agencies – all the major organisations in the city. Thirdly, a multi-sector approach is required. A competitiveness strategy for a city needs to embrace not only physical development but also business and people development. Real estate upgrading alone is not sufficient – it may simply redistribute existing economic activity. Fourthly, there should be a focus on competitiveness. The *raison d'etre* of the whole approach is to encourage and develop the competitiveness of the city within an internationally competitive environment.

Competitive strategy with six themes

Our competitive strategy for Glasgow has six development themes. Some addresses weaknesses; others build on proven strengths. The basic thrust of the strategy is that if the opportunities within each development theme (represented by key regenerator projects) are successfully exploited, then Glasgow will reposition itself at the top of Division 2 in Europe.

The Productive City: key projects seek to substantially remedy the supply-side weaknesses of the city economy and thereby improve business performance and enhance skills. *The City of Knowledge*: projects seek to make Glasgow an international centre of learning, research and development by addressing a strength – the city's knowledge industries. *The Communicating City*: Glasgow's peripheral location requires that the communications infrastructure is of a standard that does not constrain the development of business into new, particularly international, markets. *The Creative City*: projects seek to strengthen the performance of the cultural industries and increase their role in wealth creation and to contribute to the innovative vitality of related sectors. *The Liveable City*: projects aim to create a good quality urban environment. Increasingly where people choose to live will determine where companies will locate, develop, and expand. Finally, *The Humane City*: projects will be primarily directed towards those people and communities which have been marginalised by structural economic change in the city – the long term unemployed, the illiterate, the homeless, the emerging underclass.

That is a view of how Glasgow is seeking to design its future. But Glasgow is only one of a whole raft of cities in the industrialised world undergoing radical change – to its economy, to its built form and social patterns. This is a period of great uncertainty regarding future possibilities. As if to underline this uncertainty, we refer to the times we are living in as post-something: we are variously post-industrial, post-modern, post-affluent. Emphatically post-something, but post-what? Clearly the restructured economy has not yet emerged and we are still in the midst of transition – but in transit to what?

Maybe cities are always in a transitional phase. Maybe they're always in a process of what Schumpeter called 'creative destruction'. My concern here is not so much with capital cities which probably have sufficient critical mass and political and economic momentum to see them through the next generation – nor with those major cities which have been or will be beneficiaries of massive 'once-in-a-lifetime' investment (such as the Olympic Games). My concern is with the major provincial industrial cities.

In this transitional period, cities will follow different paths. There will be 'reactive' or 'accidental' cities which take their future for granted and simply react to changing external forces. City development here becomes the art of muddling through. These 'accidental' cities are unlikely to have sufficient resilience to successfully negotiate the further change and adaptation that lies ahead.

But other cities will be proactive. They will seek to become more autonomous – what Richard Knight calls 'intentional' – with increased understanding of the changing forces that underlie their future development. Those cities which are successful in the transition in the next century will see the city take shape around profound qualitative change rather than quantitative change. Cities will have less people and probably less territory – they are being 'thinned out'. Industrial cities, as their name implies, have been product-oriented and not people-oriented – and it shows. This will have to change or some cities will perish.

Over the next decade the successful cities will have to get two things right. First, economic performance: cities are the engines of regional development; indeed, to misquote Adam Smith, cities are the wealth of nations; and yet over the past generation Britain's provincial cities have become the 'sleeping giants' of the British economy – they have not contributed sufficiently to national economic performance and yet they have the potential to do so. The key question now: how are they going to do that and re-establish themselves?

Second, successful cities will be good places to live, work and visit. Increasingly, those cities where people of talent and skill choose to live will be those places where businesses will want to be. Simple proximity to transport nodes will not be sufficient; increasingly, successful business will need to be close to talent. The need is therefore to create an amenity-rich environment in order to recruit, develop and retain talent. Cities will need to be 'people-oriented' in the quality of services provided by the private and public sectors, from the quality of educational, social and cultural services to the quality of buildings and public spaces. The key challenge of the next decade is to make the industrial city a place which is both commercially competitive and attractive to live in.

City culture pays

Janice Kirkpatrick SCOTLAND

Janice Kirkpatrick graduated in graphic design and design theory from the Glasgow School of Art in 1983, founding Glasgow-based multi-disciplinary consultancy Graven Images with partner Ross Hunter. Recent projects have included the design of *The Herald,* Scotland's biggest-selling quality newspaper. Kirkpatrick now teaches part-time at the Glasgow School of Art, lectures in the UK and overseas and is working in collaboration with Glasgow Museums and the Design Council, Scotland, on the Glasgow Design Triennale.

City culture means more than opera or ballet. It is a reflection of the rich patterns of urban living and its economic benefits cannot be measured by money alone. Designers are well equipped to manage cultural strategies because of the sensorial language of symbols, signs, myths and values they employ.

Second class cities, like Glasgow, manifest their culture and personality in different ways from capital cities and first class cities. Capital cities and first class cities grew to be powerful places because they were seats of governments or centres of trade, or because they were in the correct time zone to trade in world markets, or because they became financial centres like New York, or centres of national and religious government, like Rome. They all have major command and control functions in a national and world arena.

These cities articulate their culture through monolithic objects and institutions; through tangible representations of power evident in their urban plan and architecture; through their rich cultural heritage and history; Paris, Madrid, London and New York, through their boulevards and monumental spaces, their skylines, seats of government and national resources.

Second class cities, in a European league, are not national capitals, but regional capitals. Cities with a population of a million people or more, usually controlled by a central government: Antwerp, Rotterdam, Barcelona, Milan and Lyon. Second class cities have to articulate their culture though activities. They are often post-industrial cities with less monolithic yet rich and complex architecture and heritage. They tended historically to make their culture evident through the production and movement of products, through manufacturing and trade.

A latent energy exists in many second class cities which have been through large-scale social, industrial and technological change: in Barcelona, but not Madrid; in Rotterdam but not Amsterdam; in Glasgow but not London. When Glasgow was awarded the title of 'Cultural Capital of Europe' in 1990, it was recognised there was a buzz in the city. Timing was crucial, the 80s boom was drawing to a close, there was a pulse, an energy, a dynamism which was difficult to quantify but nevertheless evident. Culture is more than the opera, ballet, symphony orchestra and national gallery. These are manifestations of state power, playing the role of international ambassadors. They have a limited repertoire and have more to do with power politics than mirroring and celebrating cultural difference. They exist not only for art's sake but to reinforce a dominant political and cultural view. High culture, state culture, is usually heavily subsidised through government, through national and international industries anxious to make their aspirations tangible, palatable to us and more civilised through association with the higher morality of art.

Popular culture, low culture, in contrast has always had to subsidise its own activities. Popular music, football, local theatre, film, art and design are paid for by the people who support them and the creative individuals, the artists, who dedicate their lives to performing and making. We all participate in cultural activity and we must expect to pay for it if we are to have a vigorous and whole society. It is the people who pay for the culture who really matter, the culture which changes lives and the fates of nations, which can give rise to the new and the innovative. We should therefore be more organised and attuned to our cultural needs in order to make the very most of our cities. All we do in our lives is cultural activity. Cities are concentrated manifestations of cultural activity.

The intangibility of culture

Culture is one of those words which everyone uses but is rarely understood. Even academics have great difficulty in coming to terms with its definition. Because culture is largely intangible it cannot be measured, it can only be interpreted. Cultural traits are qualitative by nature, and as such need to be interpreted and explained in order to be understood. It is argued that culture should be seen as a set of solutions to the key problems of survival.

Every city and every community within a city has different ways of living. These differences are articulated through everyday rituals, through art, sport, buildings, environment, products and services. These differences are unique and precious and should be explored and celebrated. They are more important and their expression more fragile than state culture because they give us a sense of identity and depend on the support of ordinary people, not governments, for their survival.

In business, cultural differences offer advantages in an increasingly competitive marketplace, giving a distinct edge which cannot be quantified in monetary terms along. Cultural differences can do the same for cities; through exploring indigenous forms of architecture; through shaping the environment to reflect the demands of people; through employing people in cultural industries – not only in the theatre and art gallery but by looking at history, community, economics and industry; through intelligently developing new industries to fill the place of the old ones. By developing cultural strategies through consultation with the wider community, designers can help gently re-orientate people away from the old culture of heavy industry, using the old power, the old ideologies, the old cultural grammar. Instead they can give meaning to a new future in an new environment with a new set of values.

Designers are particularly well equipped to understand and articulate culture, bringing forth order from apparent chaos. Designers use a sensorial vocabulary, a truly international language which utilises language, symbols, rituals, myths and values in order to control and manipulate the world around us.

The core of any culture is its ideologies. These are the fundamental driving forces which impel people into action. Because culture is largely invisible, clues have to be discovered from tangible artifacts, then interpreted. These clues are like the layers of skin on an onion which hide and protect the ideologies. There are five layers through which one has to penetrate before an understanding of ideologies can be reached: language, semiotics, myths, rituals and values.

Language

Language is more than vocabulary, it is an enabling mechanism which explains why and how people behave. It is more than what you say but how you say it. Typography acts as a container for language, giving it a new meaning, a language about a language. As communication gets faster and faster, we have an increasing need to develop new typography to describe our changing world and changing means of communication. We also need to design new ways of communicating to express our cultural differences through spoken, written and digital means and allow everyone access to a means of communication.

Semiotics

The language of signs has been described as comprising three main categories of sign: symbol, icon and index. This is an important distinction for all of us who use visual and sensorial language and we should be aware of the impact these three forms of sign can have as they change with culture and therefore need to be constantly updated and recalibrated. Symbols are abstract manifestations of a particular reality one may be trying to communicate. They are most useful in an international context when written language would not be understood. Icons are normally representational and figurative in form. They tend literally to be a mirror image of the concept being communicated. Their particular power means that they can be easily remembered. Glasgow, and Scotland, in keeping with its mythology, has lots of pictures of people showing you how to drink alcohol.

Indices are devices which engage in enigmatic surrealism. They are the most powerful of all the signs because they have the potential to penetrate our consciousness. Some of the most emotive forms of indices in use in Glasgow and the West of Scotland are colours and very simple patterns adopted by football teams and religious factions.

Myths and rituals

Claude Levi-Strauss (b 1945) declared that a myth is 'universal primitive non-rational logic'. Behind the stories embedded in myths are messages wrapped up in code. Myths are especially powerful because they don't have to be true to be believed: industry and the economy base much of their speculation on myth. Scotland and Glasgow are rich in myths.

Rituals are a necessary part of all human existence because they perform the vital role of dramatising order. As humans we cannot easily tolerate ambiguity and uncertainty for prolonged periods of time so we create systems of behaviour which will deliver an environment which provides predictability and stability. Although rituals are potent they are usually enshrined in invisible social boundaries which are often only revealed to the outsider when they are violated.

The Orange Walk is a frightening example of how behaviour is ritualised. It is really an expression of religious bigotry as well as being an extension of show business. It gives big set piece performances through the city's processional routes and traditional Catholic areas and has a continuous performance in the bars and Orange Lodges along Paisley Road West near Rangers Football Club. Architecture, design and art provide the theatrical backdrop for these performances and influence and control their shape.

Irn Bru soft drinks brand: symbol of Scottish myth-making

Values

All relationships are about values, business is about values, cities embody certain values. Values are concerned with the fundamental driving forces which impel people and cities into action. Glaswegians get passionate about right and wrong, they have a strong sense of morality and argue over education, religion, human rights, politics and football. They favour the underdog. All social and business relationships are value driven and research clearly shows that people do business with those they like rather than with those who only offer economic or technical effectiveness.

The sensorial language which designers employ can help identify, interpret and communicate the fundamental driving forces which shape city culture. Design can go some way towards revealing cultural differences, giving us an

The Rotunda, Glasgow: symbol of urban regeneration

interpretation of why Glasgow is different from other cities and how we can help reveal and enhance these differences for human and economic benefit. For economic benefit is founded in much, much more than money alone.

By revealing the underlying ideologies which underpin all city culture, by interpreting and manipulating language, symbols, myths, rituals and values through design we can recognise and understand what has happened in the past and build a framework through which we can guide our city's future development.

Culture does yield economic gain. Various means of qualitative and quantitative measurement suggest that Glasgow gained £219 million from its initial financial investment of £60 million during its year as Cultural Capital of Europe. Of that financial investment £10 million came directly from sponsorship, an extraordinarily high amount. What is not clear is the investment in terms of the people who made Glasgow's Renaissance happen. How much is a life worth? How much is quality of life worth? Now we must develop a science, a vocabulary, with the help of design and its terminologies, which will allow us to secure funding and support for people and networks rather than capital projects and specific events. If we are to continue to mine our rich cultural deposits we must ensure we protect and sustain the very people who live in our cities and make it all happen.

References

Eco, U *The Language of Semiotics* (Macmillan, London, 1977)

Lowe, A, and Hunter R, B, 'Design and Marketing Management in Innovation' *Perspectives on Marketing Management* (Wiley, Chichester, 1992)

Kirkpatrick, J and Lowe, A 'Creative Corporate Control' *Advista Arabia III* (Cairo 1992)

Kinchin, P and Kinchin, J *Glasgow's Great Exhibitions* (White Cockade, Bicester, 1988)

MacDougall, C Glasgow's *Glasgow: The Words and The Stones* (The Words and The Stones, Glasgow, 1990)

Horsey, M *Tenements and Towers* (HMSO, 1990)

Section 3:
New pathways for design

A large part of Design Renaissance was taken up with presenting new methodologies, strategies and approaches for both design education and practice. Speakers and delegates wanted to discuss solutions, not just problems. A central theme of these 'new pathways' – which are discussed by the essays in this section – revolve around the notion of bringing more intellectual depth and credibility to the design profession. **Helen Rees**, in exploring what makes a 'renaissance designer' in the modern context, refers to the spirit of intellectual enquiry that guided the original movement. **Sir Graham Hills** proposes the creation of a new type of postgraduate degree in the generics of design as the first stage in giving the subject more academic respectability in universities. **Katherine McCoy** calls for graphic design education to re-engage with social, political and moral issues after a generation in which the scientific objectivity of the Modernist agenda has marginalised designers by detaching them from content, while **Daniel Weil** argues that the academic 'laboratory for experiment' can provide new ideas in a way not possible within the commercial framework of the industrial design profession. The need for new pathways extends far beyond our schools of design – and involves new alliances. **Larry Keeley's** proposal of a generic design response to organisational strategy implies a new relationship with the management client. **Jordi Montana's** analysis of the work of DDI, the Spanish state agency, reflects a new relationship between design and government.

A renaissance in design education

Sir Graham Hills SCOTLAND

Professor Sir Graham Hills was Principal and Vice-Chancellor of the University of Strathclyde in Glasgow from 1980-91. He sits on the board of the BBC as National Governor for Scotland, and is also a member of the Board of Scottish Enterprise and a former member of the British Design Council. He is an advocate of educational reform and has worked for the redefinition and enhancement of design education. He is the President of the Design and Industries Association (DIA).

Design occupies a lowly place in the educational firmament because it appears to lack intellectual content. It pays a high price for straddling the fault line between knowledge and skill. Rescuing the subject from academic obscurity starts with defining what a good postgraduate design course should teach.

I spent most of my life lecturing to undergraduates and sometimes to my fellow academics on subject matter about which I could claim I knew quite a bit. Often I knew a great deal. Very occasionally I thought I knew more than anyone else present or for that matter anywhere else. That was the way of academic life, that was the way to climb the greasy pole of academic achievement. To know more and more about less and less. That was the only way, and in the end I felt that the only person I could hold a sensible conversation with was myself. That's when the jokes about professors begin, such as those inaudible at the back of the lecture theatre and incomprehensible at the front. Professors were people who talk in other people's sleep. Inevitably there would be a professor who dreamt he was giving a bad lecture and woke up to discover he was.

I say all this to warn you that I am not a designer and never have been. My knowledge of it is small. I have nevertheless rubbed shoulders with many designers, real and theoretical. As a vice-chancellor, I was responsibly for departments of architecture and of engineering design. I have tried to discuss with these professors its essentials on many occasions, all of which made me want to have a better understanding of this important subject. There are, of course, rare occasions when a complete outsider brings fresh thoughts and even some words of wisdom to a subject. This may well be *not* one of them, in which case I apologise in advance for what I am going to say.

I want to suggest that design as a subject to be taught or learned at present lacks enough intellectual content to make it a credible discipline in most of further and higher education. It seems to me to languish between, on the one hand, the arts and their skills, and on the other hand, the realms of knowledge and technology which are a dominant feature of most education. Throughout this paper I shall be talking about design in its broader sense, encompassing not just graphic design but product design and process design – hardware design as well as software design. The bases of my argument are as follows.

Design occupies a lowly status in the educational firmament. By and large, it has not been taught in universities, except as a poor adjunct to engineering. Rather, it has invariably been taught as a branch of graphics in art and design in literally hundreds of small centres. It is popular, well taught but it is not design in its broadest sense.

Official bodies in Britain such as the Science and Engineering Research Council and the Design Council have argued strongly about the need to produce better design and better designers, but they do little to clarify how this should be done. The importance of good design to manufacturing effectiveness and efficiency is evident to any intelligent observer of Britain's mind-numbing negative trade balance. A report published recently by the Advisory Committee of Science and Technology had some trenchant things to say about the influence of human factors and organisational design on the success of UK industry. Since production is increasingly machine based and generally automated, most of the intellectual input and all of the added value stems from the initial design of the product and the processes to make it. So why then, does design figure fleetingly in undergraduate courses and even in schools?

Design education lacking intellectual content

I believe that the answer to that question is that it is difficult at present to insert design into other undergraduate courses or school programmes because it apparently lacks 'substance'. I translate this here to mean intellectual content. Because it nevertheless remains a vital area of education and training, it might be helpful to redefine design and design education. Uncertainties about design and the way it is taught stem, in my opinion, from a fundamental misunderstanding of the meaning and nature of design.

In English, the word design takes two meanings depending on whether it is used as a *noun* or as a *verb*. Design as a noun is invariably prefaced by an adjective. Together they describe an important initial step in the manufacture of many commodities for example, aero engine design or clothes design. The noun together with its adjective are self-explanatory and seldom need further clarification. Together they describe a hands-on professional activity, like surgery or music making, which improves with practice and is best learned on the job under the eye of a master. The essential nature of this practice is common to all professions and is different from the formal classroom learning involved in most of higher and further education.

Design is also a *verb*, a stand-alone word describing the process of creating a design. It is clearly a complex association of needs, ideas, opportunities, choice, materials, shapes, value, cost, ease of making, markets and quality, to name but a few. These aspects are common to *all* designing in all contexts and constitute the intellectual skills of design – the generic basis of design. They can clearly be taught and learned in the classroom, *as well as* in the studio and laboratory. They may involve (although I think not) intrinsic attitudes or sympathies (as with music), but the basic essentials can be described and learned so that intending designers have a platform of general knowledge and general skills on which to build their professional practice, described by the adjective.

However, being a widely spread mixture of other disciplines, design in its verb form appears marginal or superficial when compared with the main subject disciplines which are focused, coherent, lead to degrees and are supported by considerable bodies of research. The phrase 'Jack-of-all-trades, master of none' fits design like a glove. Moreover, as with drama, art and architecture, the inspirational character of design is difficult to measure or examine. In its hand-waving form, it looks a soft option. For all these reasons and more, design is not a regular, respectable discipline of higher education.

Knowledge versus skill in education

To appreciate the importance of these distinctions, we need to ask some questions about education itself. What follows is a major but necessary digression into the nature of teaching and learning itself. Broadly, the business of higher and further education falls into three distinct categories of effort: the efforts to acquire knowledge – the know what; skills – the do what; and technology – the know how.

Of these, the most important is technology. It is the solver of all problems. It is the creator of all wealth but it is not well regarded or valued. It is down market and thought to be the source of all of our problems. On the other hand, knowledge is overwhelmingly the most upmarket. From its classical Greek origins knowledge is the acme of achievement. To be called knowledgeable is to be complimented. To be called skilled less so. To be called a technologist is a faint insult.

In the UK, the distinction between knowledge and its adherents and skills and its practitioners is sharp and painful. Everywhere in our education are devices (normally called examinations) designed to separate thinkers from doers; white collars from blue collars; white coats from overalls; philosophers and mathematicians from plumbers and sculptors; and people who write and talk about music from those who actually play it, and so on and so on. It is the singular misfortune of design to straddle the fault line between these two worlds.

I have no wish to score political points about Britain's imperial past, its class structures, its elitist system of higher education, its obsession with the written word, with abstract thought and with theories. But the catalogue is endless and we can have no sensible discussion of education – higher, lower, further, tertiary, secondary, or primary – without understanding its framework of values and prejudices.

The relevance of all this to design which has a relatively small knowledge content, is that design is automatically cast into outer darkness and as yet finds no place in higher education. It is not the only waif. Engineering itself, very much a skill-based activity, has a hard job to stay on the right side of the divide. The social sciences with their rather wobbly knowledge bases are also always in danger of being outcasts.

Some subjects, entirely skills-based, have made it into high respectability by being nearer to the bone, real or otherwise. Dentistry, surgery, medicine in general and especially the law require skills and lots of practice, and by clever use of restrictive practices they are in the lifeboat. Musicians and physiotherapists have a harder time.

Other subject areas with seemingly scant regard for knowledge, such as economics, politics and management, have protected their patch with a healthy infusion of theoretical material with lots of isms. Theory is often and wilfully confused with knowledge. It is one road to success seemingly closed to design, the theoretical content of which is exceedingly small.

Others still cling to their success by means of scarcity. Knowledge owes its high esteem to the fact that its disciples by-and-large kept it to themselves and made it difficult for outsiders to intrude. This was the essence of the resistance of the Catholic Church to the translation of The Bible into English. Many went to the stake in their efforts to do so.

But the edifice of educational achievements bolstered by excluding tests and examinations is the direct descendant of the Guildry by which the tradesmen of the Middle Ages established their position in the face of the Church and the nobility. It is hardly noticeable in the USA. It is particularly noticeable in England.

Citadel of knowledge is crumbling

Today this hierarchy is crumbling in the UK. The exclusivity of higher education is on the way out. The league tables of success, the pressures to get into Oxbridge will sort themselves out as more and more universities and colleges establish their niches in the field of tertiary education. The higher education age participation rate, scarcely 10 per cent in 1980, is now rising to 30 per cent and perhaps even 40 per cent. Halfway to the Japanese level. Two specific things are also happening. First, because of the move to vocational studies, the importance of skills in relation to knowledge will increase. Human skills of all kinds will be learned and valued as machines take over the routine knowledge-based activities. Second, the knowledge base itself has exploded and is in every subject well beyond the capacity of the human mind to encompass. At the same time, the capacity for computer storage, especially on hard disc, has become infinite. The knowledge base is rapidly becoming universal and universally accessible. The new values are to be found not in knowledge retention but in the packaging of the knowledge base. The downside of too much knowledge is now evident in obsession and nihilism. Knowledge is luggage and one should travel light.

These developments are having a profound effect on education as a whole. The virtuous cycle of learning has been redefined and the role that was once the preserve and *raison d'etre* of the teacher is the one role best done by the computer workstation and its CD ROM package. Thus didactic teaching has become knowledge transmission, soon to be the province of the tutorial workshop and studio. Assessment, prescription and motivation are the province of one-to-one encounters between the student and teacher. Perhaps it is now the right time to return to design. Given what has gone before, we can ask the question 'how far is design a knowledge-based subject or a skills-based subject?' In our bones we know it has to be both but we should not stuff it with apparently useful knowledge just to make it respectable or academically acceptable.

It is inevitable that professional needs will dictate a substantial knowledge content as part of the education and training of the specialist designer. Within that knowledge envelope it is then possible to practise the specialist *skills* required to develop and apply that knowledge in the studio, in the workshop, at the workstation or in the laboratory. But that is where we are now with design as a noun and we have to ask whether design as such (the verb) can be more.

Putting the customer ahead of the mechanic

Because engineering design is so important to manufacturing, more has been written and said about design in this area than anywhere else. Stuart Pugh's book *Total Design* (Wokingham, Addison-Wesley, 1990) is the fruit of a lifetime's endeavour to persuade engineers to put the customer's needs first and the mechanic's second. Marketing is not the first subject taught to budding engineers. Generally it is not taught to them at all, hence Concorde and Clive Sinclair's C5 Banana Car. But clearly courses in design can be progressively enriched with other subjects of interest and relevance to the budding designer. The business skills of marketing, managing and financial control spring to mind as important to anyone entering the world of design. Computer literacy has become so important that, like driving a car and operating a word processor, we should also enjoy a high level of computational and keyboard skills. Should everyone be familiar with the nature of materials from silk to wood to concrete and stainless steel? The list of add-on extras is formidable.

So one way to broaden the appeal and usefulness of design education is simply to broaden the range of material. Given the modular nature of most undergraduate courses, the relationship of the new subject material to the design core of the course can then be strengthened by projects or case-studies illustrating the value of the connection. The new subjects can be integrated prescriptively or cafeteria-style depending on student choices and options. The case of design engineering is the easiest to illustrate. Extra options are being vigorously pressed into the engineering syllabus by the Royal Academy of Engineering and other such professional bodies in Britain. The design content (the noun) would be that of the supporting subjects. The design process (the verb) would be that of their integration into a complete design operation. The engineering designer would then emerge as a person with an inclination to join a design office and begin the process of learning by example.

If the same is true for all other products and processes, where then are the generic elements of design which we can hold up to the young and say 'this is the way'? If we don't do that then we run the risk of the brightest and the best (however we might define these words) reading instead, *as they do now* English, Philosophy, Politics, Economics and all the other specialist subjects reaching down into the schools and the schools literature.

Another aside has to do with our not-very-good performance in manufacturing industry. It may not be that we are not so good at this as we wish, but simply that the offspring of the great, the good, the rich, the well-connected, the likely winners in any race, simply aren't attracted to industry before it is too late to do anything about it. This matter is greatly exacerbated by the narrowing requirements of 'A' levels and their evil encouragement, in England at least, of early specialisation.

A new model for design education
So what can we do to rescue design from that fate? We must give it a corpus of coherent knowledge that defines the meaning and therefore the generic bases of design as such. That is the challenge. It has first to be defined at the top where the subjects begin. If we cannot define at the Masters level what a good postgraduate course in design should include, then we will not persuade any university to adopt design as an undergraduate option, or any school to treat it as a serious A level alternative to History, Economics or a science major.

My list of contents will not be definitive. It may be rank amateurish but here goes. I have listed eight areas of current interest and importance (opposite). They are a mixture of enabling technologies and defining frameworks. The course should attempt to emulate the success of the MBA and of the burgeoning courses on the management of technology.

This course we shall describe as Design and Management because design is not yet strong enough a word to stand alone. It should be a flagship course in flagship institutions and be suitable for anyone wishing to enter design from an arts-based, science-based, technology-based or business-based background.

A few graduate schools should be established to service the degree. They should buy as many as possible of the separate courses from other specialist providers, leaving the course leaders, the design tutors and members to supervise the integrative course projects, all of them based on case studies and developments of them. The course would be strengthened by frequent workshops with professional designers.

There will be no sketching, making or toying with materials. This is a course of high intellectual content meant to go with talents and skills already there or being formed elsewhere. In its refined form, it can then be offered as an honours option in certain undergraduate courses. Even if honours degree courses evolve into largely general foundation courses then there would still be opportunities for attractive design options.

It may be asking too much to create such a new combination from so many different sources but I do not see how else it can be done, slowly or otherwise. Design needs a rebirth with a big bang, not in schools, not even in colleges and universities, but in high places such as graduate schools.

The comprehensive integrating nature of design is its outstanding feature. It stands against the narrowing tendencies of the individual disciplines. The more and more about less and less which is where I came in. We are supposed to be a clever people, intensively knowledgeable and we have a great advantage that all

A Master Course in the Generics of Design
Suitable for any person wishing to qualify to enter one
of the design professions.

1. A visual history of design and designers. Notable successes and failures.

2. The bases of perception, choice and taste. The essentials of marketing, market research, advertising and selling.

3. Linear programming, algorithms, decision trees, operational research and elementary statistics.

4. Information technology, databases, computer simulation, CAD, virtual realities.

5. History of technology, its economic and political impact.

6. The nature of culture: values, ethics, opinions, traditions and change.

7. The nature of materials and artifacts, shape, form, perspective, painting, sculpture, pottery, furniture, printing, weaving and sewing.

8. The management of people and systems. People, technology and organisations. Human factors and organisational design.

new knowledge is in our language. We should be amongst the leaders in design but I believe we must do better for its own sake as well as for the economy.

In one respect, design is like politics. It seeks to find real solutions to real problems in a way which the arts and the sciences don't have to confront. It is like politics in that it has to take into account every aspect of its problem. To miss just one might result in catastrophic failure. Design therefore is the greatest of challenges, both in its intellectual content and in its skills. If we can redefine that intellectual challenge, then design as such will have been reborn.

Generic design strategies

Larry Keeley USA

Larry Keeley is a strategic planner who has focused for nearly 15 years on the strategic value of design for larger corporations. He is President of Doblin Group, the world's largest strategic design planning firm. Clients include Aetna, Mexican Hospital Supply, Amoco, Steelcase, and Xerox. Keeley is a frequent lecturer on design, a board member of the American Centre for Design, and a past board member for the Design Management Institute.

Organisational strategy has a set of theories which are stable and broadly accepted. So why has the design field never forged a parallel theory in response? Most designers accept whatever strategy they are handed, but they have the power to reshape industries through a generic strategy model.

Fourteen years ago, Michael Porter posited three generic strategies[1] for organisations. Porter's simple, powerful assertion was that all organisational strategies cluster into three large patterns: *least cost manufacturer*, enabling an organisation to undercut the prices of all direct competitors without suffering loss of margin; *differentiation,* suggesting some capability customers value that competitive organisations cannot emulate, typically leading to higher prices without loss of market share; and *focus*, suggesting the ability to serve some segment of an overall industry in ways that are more efficient, more effective, or both, typically leading to above average margins and protected market share within a niche.

Porter's seminal work has gone largely unchallenged ever since. It remains the academic foundation for organisational strategy theory at Harvard Business School (where Porter teaches) and at other leading business schools worldwide.

The stability and broad acceptance of this theory makes it all the more remarkable that the design field has never forged a parallel theory in response. Two obvious questions are begged: if there are only three generic organisational strategies, what can the design field do to contribute to each? Separately, are there some generic design strategies that can be understood and fostered by advanced design methods?

Doblin Group sought to ask and answer these questions in its internal r&d programme for 1993. What we found was fascinating. By comparing and analysing hundreds of successful design projects we found patterns in the kinds of value design typically adds.

This leads us to posit seven common design objectives. But since these were *derived* from projects where design is typically relegated to some minor role we sought to look deeper as well. As we did, we tried to develop a model for ways that design can help fundamentally alter the strategic balance of an industry, leading to breakthrough success for some player. This causes us to assert four generic design strategies, each able to reshape markets.

These generic design strategies are the second of two major design strategy theories Doblin Group has authored. They are often useful in tandem. The 1993 research leads to an effective 'macro radar': it should help companies broadly scan for directions that can reshape an entire field and radically alter the competitive balance. A second approach to strategy, Doblin Group's 1991 Strategic Palette[2], can reliably provide insights into design advances at a more micro level, say for a product line or business unit.

Creating an advantage

At the business schools, strategy is fundamentally about *value creation*. In pragmatic terms, good strategies always lead to some kind of advantage; by appealing to customers, by differentiating a company, or by outmaneuvering competitors. Truly great strategies are rare indeed. They manage to defeat competitors almost automatically. Lexus today, combining a great product with uniquely personal and low pressure sales approaches, and extraordinary service after the sale, is systematically destroying market share for Jaguar, Mercedes, BMW and Porsche. This is integrated, powerful and well-executed *strategy*.

Strategy is an issue today because of the pace and complexity of modern business dynamics. It is clear that changes are happening in most major industries to a degree and at a rate that is completely unprecedented, exceeding even the time of the Industrial Revolution. In this environment, winners can become losers very rapidly, as IBM, GM and Sears will all attest. Moreover, unknown players can reshape entire industries, as CNN has demonstrated in broadcasting and Home Shopping Club has shown for retailing.

Designers and strategy

Most designers accept whatever strategy they are handed. This is a common and classic mistake. People at the high end of design practice are now directly shaping strategy. This normally requires special teams and methods but it is possible because designers are skilled in contributing three basic ways.

First they focus on and care about end-users of an artefact, a habit often lacking amongst other professionals. Second, they have conceptual skills about changing artefacts, an ability that can be hugely rewarded today. Third, they can *simulate* things that don't exist yet in ways that permit other individuals with less imagination to experience them. At Doblin Group, we argue that designers, acting at the concept level, can play a vital role in helping to conceive, shape and clarify strategy.

If strategy is fundamentally about creating value, one obvious question to ask is: what kinds of value can be added through good design? To search for an answer to this question, Doblin Group began by taking hundreds of successful products and services and analysing them to discern the role played by design. Proprietary clustering methods were used to find patterns in design contributions.

The net result was a discovery of seven essential design tactics, shown below as a tree structure. We call these *tactics* for the simple reason that none of them used alone is likely to be powerful enough to create a strategic breakthrough. Indeed, consider an interesting piece of logic. These tactics were *derived* by examining contributions of design and designers, but designers are usually directed by others and given proscribed roles. Therefore, these clusters only show the best contributions designers probably tend to make, not the best they are capable of making.

Despite these limitations, the seven basic design tactics are interesting. It is also interesting that they cluster into two larger sets; four tactics relate to *users* and three relate to *markets*. Done well, any of these, or especially combinations of them, can play an important role in supporting a powerful strategy.

Design tactics model

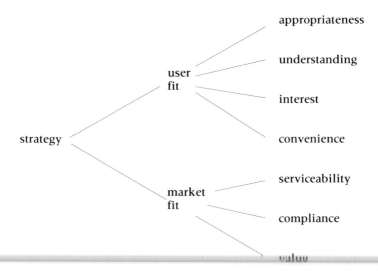

Frontiers of strategy

Strategy is taught and shaped through *frameworks*, Porter's strategy framework described earlier being one of the most popular. Increasingly these frameworks are commonplace and universal. They are taught and applied broadly at the world's leading business schools, at most consulting firms, and within large corporations. It is increasingly possible that the wide dispersion of common frameworks is itself a cause now of strategies in decline. Two leading theorists, C K Prahalad and Gary Hamel are attacking this directly, and have authored an important series of four articles in *Harvard Business Review* that try to move thought processes about strategy beyond the ordinary.

In their most recent paper, 'Strategy as Stretch and Leverage'[3], Hamel and Prahalad argue that managers acquire managerial frames of reference 'invisibly, from business school and other educational experience, from peers, consultants, and the business press, and above all, from their own career experiences'. They go on to say that these invisible 'frames' become the assumptions, premises and accepted wisdom that bound a company's understanding of itself and its industry and drive competitive strategy.

In effect, these are the hidden beliefs and assumptions that tell us what it means to be 'strategic'. Too often they are limiting. With startling regularity, the frameworks themselves are wrong and executives are insufficiently aware of what is possible, desirable and achievable.

By analysing patterns in the contributions of design, then by analysing commonplace weaknesses in organisational strategies, Doblin Group is now prepared to assert and defend a *generic strategy model*. In essence this work provides a map that encourages broad conceptual thinking about what can be done to fundamentally reshape industries. This model balances both organisational and end-user issues, and can be used in three basic ways: first, analytically, to determine who's winning and losing within a given market at any point in time and why; second, analytically, to look at a market to discern its transformations over time; and third, prescriptively, to help look forward and predict or shape transformations that are relevant to users and likely to significantly alter the strategic balance.

Generic strategies model

new framework

	INTEGRATE CONCEPT Walkman Lexus Books on Tape Swatch Disposable camera Starbucks Wal-Mart	INVENT CONCEPT Post-it Notes Polaroid CNN QVC, HSC Digital imaging Madonna	
current capabilities			new capabilities
	IMPROVE CONCEPT Micro-Tac Phone Gillette Sensor Home Depot Call-Waiting DCC	EXTEND CONCEPT Newman's Own Disney Electric cars Nintendo	

current framework

The effective use of this model requires careful understanding of its underlying structure. Throughout the model, the goal is to achieve *transformational change.* We define this as the ability to fundamentally alter an industry. Thus, *Improve Concept* in the lower left hand box, seemingly the easiest change to achieve, is only good enough if the resulting offering is *ten times better* than other substitutes available within a market. Thus, anything good enough to make this map is very good indeed. Throughout the model, *conceptual* challenges should be expected. It is applied most effectively by special design research methods and teams.

The horizontal axis is about *capabilities.* Changing capabilities might mean the ability of an organisation to change the kinds of products it makes, the properties of those products, its services, its processes, its positioning, brand expectations, and so on. Normally there are many barriers within an organisation to this type of change. Such changes, if achieved, may yield market advances for two to five years before competitors catch up. Often portions of these advances are subject to patent protection, permitting, when you are very lucky, a partial advantage for perhaps 15 years.

The vertical axis is about *frameworks.* These are those vexing, invisible sets of hidden assumptions that blind both organisations and their customers to what might be possible. Changing frameworks is really tough. This may require changes to customer expectations, channel behaviours, service and sales practices, information systems, and more. Such changes, if achieved, can often disrupt a market balance for four to ten years before competitors catch up.

The four generic design strategies can be described in a nutshell:

- *Improve:* seeks a ten-fold improvement over the status quo
- *Extend:* transforms an existing strategy in a surprising way
- *Integrate:* combines many current capabilities systematically
- *Invent:* creates something wholly new and valued by end users

While these are different kinds of change, each yields dramatic market transformation and value creation. At a minimum, the model is a smart guide to conceptual transformation. It should help people identify and challenge their assumptions about the status quo. At its best, this model can lead to radical but relevant industry breakthroughs. When it does so, naturally it reshapes the role and economic value of designs and designers.

Beyond industry patterns

At any given time there are companies that tend to break out of the pack and move substantially beyond industry patterns. Nike, in sporting goods; Toyota and Lexus in automobiles; Microsoft in software; Sony in consumer electronics; CNN in network news broadcasting. Each of these companies has demonstrated conceptual skills in creating a strategy matched with organisational skills in executing it.

At Doblin Group we are interested in the powerful use of design to reshape industries and markets. Generic design strategies appear to offer four basic ways to *reliably* create the requisite strategies. In conjunction with user-centred research and great strategy prototyping, they can help individuals within an organisation to clearly understand what is possible in vital new ways.

Of course simulating a new strategy is a long way from achieving it. We are aware that this type of thinking and behaviour is inherently traumatising to the individuals it affects. Change management skills, a relatively new term applied to many different types of organisational development tools and processes, would normally also be required for clients to get the full value of this type of work.

References

1. Porter, Michael, *Competitive Strategy*, 1980, The Free Press, div. Macmillan Publishing Co, pp 34-46.
2. Keeley, Larry, 'The Strategic Palette', see *Communication Arts Magazine*, May/June 1992, pages 134-139, for a brief summary.
3. Hamel, Gary, and Prahalad CK 'Strategy as Stretch and Leverage', *Harvard Business Review*, March-April, 1993 pp 75-84.

An intellectual debt is owed to three research associates of Doblin Group for their assistance. Toby Bottorf, Ewan Duncan and Kimberly Erwin, all Master's degree candidates at Chicago's Institute of Design, played important roles in conceiving and shaping some of the ideas presented here.

What makes a Renaissance designer?

Helen Rees ENGLAND

Helen Rees is Head of Public Affairs at the National Art Collections Fund. Her involvement in design began with her appointment as information officer for the Conran Foundation in 1984. She was a curator at London's acclaimed Boilerhouse exhibition space at the Victoria and Albert Museum. Between 1989 and 1992 she was Director of the Design Museum, London.

Renaissance designers in the fifteenth century were not defined by artistic virtuosity alone. They took their place at the heart of an entire movement of intellectual enquiry. Today's Renaissance individuals must also search for answers to the eternal question of the role of the designer in society.

By the end of the (fifteenth) century the artist had freed himself from guild rules and might accept any commission he wished; he had become the intimate friend of leading citizens, his idiosyncrasies were tolerated, he had come to be recognised not only as a skilled technician, but as a thinker, a discoverer, an inventor...

In this way the historian Vincent Cronin describes the rise of the Renaissance artist in a *quattrocentro* Florence. Today the casual idiomatic use of the word 'Renaissance' frequently suggests an individual who has diverse talents, and whose skills and interests cross the conceptual boundaries between art and science, pure and applied.

Many designers might recognise such opportunistic versatility as prerequisite for survival in economic conditions which do not permit the luxury of specialism. Indeed, this may be one of the defining features of those designers who seek to make a living in the 1990s as consultants to, rather than working inside, industry.

In the history of twentieth century design, two characters most vividly personify the application of their talents to an extreme range of commissions. Both Raymond Loewy (1893-1986) and Philippe Starck (b1949) made ubiquity their trademark. Crossing the world, they made a fortune from vaulting the cultural, technical and educational barriers between graphic, product and building design. Yet such commercial gadflys now leave a sense of unease in their wake. Theirs is not a sustainable blueprint for the design business: speaking as a client, I would argue that drawing on the back of an envelope on the Paris-Tokyo shuttle should only be the start, rather than the end, of the design process.

Part of a larger project

Being a Renaissance designer at the end of the twentieth century means more than being willing and able to turn your hand to anything. The artists of the fifteenth century were not separated from their predecessors by artistic or commercial virtuosity alone. More importantly they were at the heart of a new movement of intellectual enquiry, which was primarily preoccupied with the rights and responsibilities of the individual in a just society. They were part of a project, led by scholars, politicians and businessmen, to understand how Christian men might live, reinvigorated by a new freedom of the mind, body and spirit which had been inspired by the rediscovery of classical texts. It was as part of this project that a new contract was forged between the artist and society.

The choice of 'Renaissance Designers' to speak at the Glasgow Design Congress was not determined by a frantic search for people who had designed a rocket, a tower block *and* a handbag, but rather for designers whose work suggested that they were actively searching for an answer to the question: what is the role of the designer at this time? Overwhelmingly, their response was that they shared much more in common as *designers,* irrespective of their field of practice. No matter *what* they designed, it was *how* and *why* they designed which connected them with each other.

Such bonds crossed geographical as well as professional frontiers. Like the artists who once travelled across Europe from city to city in search of refuge and patronage, today's designers work in an international landscape. Some, such as Eva Jiricna who is Czech, have travelled to escape oppression, while others, such as Perry King, a Briton living in Milan, pursued commercial and cultural opportunities in another country. Similarly – and despite the domination of middle-aged, male speakers throughout the congress – differences of age and gender are an inspiration, not a barrier, to the brightest designers of our times, as collaborators Lisa Krohn from the USA and Gert Dumbar from The Netherlands exemplified.

Paul Williams, who is British, remarked that he feels he can design anything, because he and his partner, Alan Stanton, bring the same purpose, principles and process to a building or a product. The point is not that he is a 'designer' in partnership with an 'architect' who together design shops exhibitions, museums and houses, but that they share consistent principles. Whatever the job, Williams' response is first to question the problem as articulated by the client: together they unpack the preconceptions which shape every brief, and only then does he begin to work on a solution. The principles of design which make a good exhibition space are the same which make a good living room; only their application is profoundly different.

Involvement in design education

The majority of the Renaissance designers who participated in Glasgow are involved in the education of students seeking to join the design business. They are not only articulate spokespeople for their business, they are actively concerned to offer their experience to the next generation. The function, perception and status of designers is obviously a reflection of the way in which they are taught and trained. It is our education systems which must answer the question: what are the requirements for designers in the late twentieth century? Similarly, schools must address the development of visual literacy in the population as a whole.

How can design courses meet the demands of the marketplace of the future: through vocational training driven by the commercial imperatives of the present, or through a liberal education which questions the central paradigm of problem-solving? In Britain, design colleges erect the walls between one design discipline and another. Higher education presents the greatest opportunity to stimulate disciplined intellectual enquiry among tomorrow's designers. Too often, in the UK at least, it is an opportunity lost. None of our Renaissance designers expressed optimism for such a system.

There is a difference between being able to identify the characteristics of a group of 'Renaissance Designers' (the title of the session I chaired) and being able to identify a 'Design Renaissance' (the title of the congress). By the time the event took place, its title, invented at the end of the booming 80s, had acquired an ironic twist. Gone are the days when the design business could just about believe in its own rhetoric. In Britain and the USA, the death of borrow-and-spend economics finally exposed the idea that designers could save the world as the embarrassing hubris it always was. And now the effects of economic recession on mainland Europe are compounded by political upheaval in the two countries whose post-war economic miracle was predicated on the value of design in manufacturing: Germany and Italy.

Meanwhile cracks in the system are exposing the fragility of Japanese corporatism. Capitalism won only a hollow victory as Marxism finally ground to a halt. Against this depressing background, our individual designers looked and sounded like beacons of intelligence and integrity in Glasgow. But if the only viable response to our common situation is a purely personal one, it is a far remove from the social impulse of the Florentine Renaissance.

Russian reference point: rock music logo in the Moscow magazine
Greatis

Retaining political and social force

The one speaker in this session who showed that design still retains its political and social force, was Serge Serov, a graphic designer from Moscow and the editor of *Greatis* magazine. In a moving address, accompanied by images of recent events in Russia, he showed how the failed putsch of August 1991 had resulted in an extraordinary series of graphic images. Through a dramatic visual presentation, he illustrated the power of design and photography to reflect and encode the meaning of direct action in the street.

Unlike the utopian visual language of the 1917 Revolution, today's designers are free to use references from Russia's distant and recent past. Religious and Czarist iconography are available for appropriation, mixed with elements of western funk: influences from Push Pin Studios, heavy metal rock graphics and fashion photography. Of course, the technological constraints on graphic designers, however severe compared with their western colleagues, are slight compared with the situation of product designers facing a massive and chaotic upheaval in Russian manufacturing industry. And even as Serov spoke in Glasgow, the storming of the Russian White House was less than four weeks away.

Like Serov, our Renaissance designers are bound by a spirit of entrepreneurialism, curiosity and internationalism. Their common frame of reference is cultural as well as industrial, and educational as well as economic. To sustain a successful business as a consultant designer requires intellectual as well as physical stamina. No one style unites them, and one suspects that their admiration for each other's products is outweighed by their respect for each other's processes.

References

1. Cronin, Vincent, *The Florentine Renaissance,* Pimlico Press 1992 (first published Collins 1967)

Countering the tradition of the apolitical designer

Katherine McCoy USA

Katherine McCoy is co-Chairman of the Department of Design at the Cranbrook Academy of Art, and a partner of McCoy & McCoy Associates. Her design practice emphasises interior design and graphic design for cultural, educational and corporate clients, including Formica, Unisys, and Philips. She writes frequently on design criticism and history and co-produced a television documentary on Japanese design.

Graphic design education and practice, shaped by the legacy of Bauhaus and Basel, has emphasised professional detachment and objective rationalism at the expense of content. But today's designers must rediscover the purpose of design as a social, moral and political force.

This decade finds us in a crisis of values in the United States. Our increasingly multicultural society is experiencing a breakdown in shared values – national values, tribal values, personal values, even family values – consensual motivating values that create a common sense of purpose in a community.

The question is how can a heterogeneous society develop shared values and yet encourage cultural diversity and personal freedom? Designers and design education are part of the problem, and can be part of the answer. We cannot afford to be passive anymore. Designers must be good citizens and participate in the shaping of our government. As designers we could use our particular talents and skills to encourage others to wake up and participate as well.

Before the US congratulates itself too much on the demise of Communism, we must remember that our American capitalist democracy is not what it used to be either. Much of our stagnation comes from this breakdown of values. Entrepreneurial energy and enthusiastic energy and enthusiastic work ethic have deteriorated into individual self-interest, complacency, corporate greed, and resentment between ethnic groups and economic classes. Our common American purpose is fading – that sense of building something new where individuals could progress through participating in a system that provided opportunity. Consumerism and materialism now seem to be the only ties that bind. The one group that seems to be bound by more than this is the Far Right; but their bond is regressive, a desire to force fundamentalist prescriptive values on the rest of us.

We have just experienced the Reagan era during which we were told it was all okay, that we could spend and consume with no price tag attached. During this period, graphic designers enjoyed the spoils of artificial prosperity with the same passive hedonism as the rest of the country. Now we are beginning to realise it was not all okay. The earth is being poisoned, its resources depleted, and the US has gone from a creditor to a debtor nation. Our self-absorbtion and lack of activism has left a void filled by minority single-issue groups aggressively pushing their concerns. There are serious threats to our civil liberties in the United States from both fundamentalist censorship of the right and political correctness from the left. We have seen the dismemberment of artistic freedom at the National Endowment for the Arts in the past three years and aggressive attempts to censor public schools' teaching from Darwin to Hemingway to safe sex. As graphic designers specialising in visual communications, the content of our communications may be seriously curtailed if we do not defend our freedom of expression.

An act of self-censorship
But even more troubling is our field's own self-censorship. How many graphic designers today would feel a loss if their freedom of expression was handcuffed? Most of our colleagues never exercise their right to communicate on public issues or potentially controversial content. Remove our freedom of speech and graphic designers might never notice. We have trained a profession that feels political or social concerns are either extraneous to our work, or inappropriate.

Thinking back to 1968, the atmosphere at Unimark International during my first year of work typified this problem. Unimark (an idealistic international design office with Massimo Vignelli and Jay Doblin as vice presidents, and Herbert Bayer on the board of directors) was dedicated to the ideal of the rationally objective professional. The graphic designer was to be the neutral transmitter of the client's messages. Clarity and objectivity were the goal.

During that year, the designers I worked with, save one notable exception, were all remarkably disinterested in the social and political upheavals taking place around us. Vietnam was escalating with body counts touted on every evening newscast; the New Left rioted before the Democratic National Convention in Chicago; Martin Luther King and Robert Kennedy were assassinated; and Detroit was still smoking from its riots just down the street from our office. Yet hardly a word was spoken on these subjects. We were encouraged to wear white lab coats, perhaps so the messy external environment would not contaminate our surgically clean detachment.

These white lab coats make an excellent metaphor for the apolitical designer, cherishing the myth of universal value-free design. They suggest that design is a clinical process akin to chemistry, scientifically, pure and neutral, conducted in a sterile laboratory environment with precisely predictable results. Yet Lawrence and Oppenheimer and a thousand other examples teach us that even chemists and physicists must have a contextual view of their work in the social/political world around them.

During that time, I became increasingly interested in the social idealism of the times: the civil rights movement, the anti-Vietnam peace movement, the anti-materialism and social experimentation of the New Left, and radical feminism. Yet it was very difficult to relate these new ideas to the design that I was practising and the communication process that I loved so much. Or perhaps the difficulty was not the values of design so much as the values of the design community. About all I could connect with was designing and sending (to appalled family members) an anti-Vietnam feminist Christmas card and silkscreening t-shirts with a geometricised 'Swiss' version of the feminist symbol. Meanwhile, we continued to serve the corporate and advertising worlds with highly 'professional' design solutions.

The implication of the word 'professional' is indicative of the problem here. How often do we hear, 'Act like a professional' or 'I'm a professional, I can handle it'. Being a professional means to put aside one's personal reactions regardless of the situation and to carry on. Prostitutes, practitioners of the so-called oldest profession, must maintain an extreme of cool objectivity about this most intimate of human activities, disciplining their personal responses to deliver an impartial and consistent product to their clients.

This ideal of the dispassionate professional distances us from ethical and political values. Think of the words used to describe the disciplined objective professional, whether it be scientist, doctor or lawyer: impartial, dispassionate, disinterested. These become pejorative terms in a difficult world crying out for compassion, interest, concern, commitment and involvement.

Disinterest is appropriate for a neutral arbitrator but not for an advocate. In fact, most often design education trains students to think of themselves as passive arbitrators of the message between the client/sender and audience/receiver, rather than as advocates for the message content or the audience's needs. Here is the challenge – how to achieve the objectivity and consistency of professionalism without stripping oneself of personal convictions.

Our concept of graphic design professionalism has been largely shaped – and generally for the better – by the legacy of twentieth century Modernism as it has come to us through the Bauhaus and Swiss lineages. However, there are several dominant aspects of this Modernist ethic that have done much to distance designers from their cultural milieu. The ideals, forms, methods and mythology of Modernism are a large part of this problem of detachment, including the paradigms of universal form, abstraction, self-referentialism, value-free design, rationality and objectivity.

A much-needed antidote

Objective rationalism, particularly that of the Bauhaus, provided a much needed antidote to the sentimentality and gratuitous eclecticism found in nineteenth century mass production, visual communications and architecture. Linked to functionalism, objective analysis formed the basis of problem-solving methods to generate functional design solutions to improve the quality of daily life. Expanded more recently to include systems design, this attitude has done much to elevate the quality of design thinking.

Linked to the ideal of the objective clear-sighted designer is the ideal of value-free universal forms. Perhaps a reaction to the frequent political upheavals between European nations, especially World War One, early Modernist designers hoped to find internationalist design forms and attitudes that would cross those national, ethnic and class barriers that had caused such strife. In addition, a universal design – one design for all – would be appropriate for the

America is Angry: poster by Richard Bates, Cranbrook Academy of Art

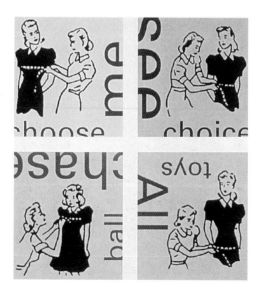

Choose Me reproductive choice poster, by Cranbrook designer Martin Venezky: a comparison between the objectification of womanhood and the removal of personal autonomy for young women

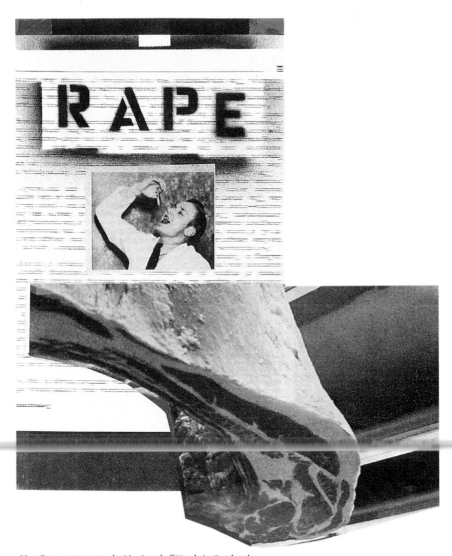

*Meat Rape protest poster: by Lisa Langhoff Voorheis, Cranbrook
Academy of Art*

classless mass society of industrial workers envisioned by early twentieth century social reformers.

But passing years and different national contexts have brought different results from the application of these Modernist design paradigms. The myth of objectivity unfortunately does much to disengage the designer from compassionate concerns. Strongly held personal convictions would seem to be inappropriate for the cool-headed objective professional. Functionalism is narrowly defined in measurable utilitarian terms. Too often this means serving the client's definition of function – generally profits – over other concerns, including safety, the environment, and social/cultural/political/environmental impacts.

Universalism has brought us an homogenised corporate style which is based mainly on Helvetica and the grid, and ignores the power and potential of regional, idiosyncratic, personal or culturally specific stylistic vocabularies. And the ideal of value-free design is a dangerous myth. In fact all design solutions carry a bias, either explicit or implicit. The more honest designs acknowledge their biases openly rather than manipulate their audiences with assurances of universal 'truth' and purity.

Abstraction, Modernism's revolutionary contribution to the visual language of art and design, further distances both designer and audience from involvement. Stripped of imagery, self-referential abstraction is largely devoid of symbols and disconnected from experience in the surrounding world. It is cool and low on emotion. Abstraction is predictable in application, polite, inoffensive and not too meaningful – thereby providing a safe vocabulary for corporate materials. Imagery, on the other hand, is richly loaded with symbolic encoded meaning, often ambiguous and capable of arousing the entire range of human emotions. Imagery is difficult to control, even dangerous or contro-versial, often leading to unintended personal interpretations on the part of the audience – but also poetic, powerful and potentially eloquent.

Tendancy to avoid political dialectics

The Modernist agenda has conspired to promote an apolitical attitude among American designers, design educators and students, building on the pragmatic American tendency to avoid political dialectics. American designers consistently take European theories and strip them of their political content. Of the various strains of Modernism, many of which were socially concerned or politically revolutionary, American design either chose those most devoid of political content or stripped the theories of their original political idealism.

More recently we have seen a strong interest in French literary theory. But its original element of French contemporary Marxism has been largely ignored in the US, perhaps rightly so. The American political environment is far different from the European; European political dialectics may not be appropriate to us. Yet we cannot assume that no political theory is needed to ground our work – all designers need an appropriate framework to evaluate and assess the impact of their work within its social/ethical/political milieu. Perhaps an appropriate evaluative framework would be different for each individual, reflecting our strong tradition of American individualism.

Designers must break out of the obedient, neutral, servant-to-industry mentality, an orientation that was particularly strong in the Reagan/Thatcher 1980s, and continues to dominate design management and strategic design. Yes, we are problem-solvers responding to the needs of clients. But we must be careful of the problems we take on. Should one help sell tobacco and alcohol, or design a Ronald Reagan Presidential memorial library for a man who reads only pulp cowboy novels? Design is not a neutral, value-free process. A design has no more integrity than its purpose or subject matter. Garbage in, garbage out. The most rarefied design solution can never surpass the quality of its content.

A dangerous assumption is that corporate work of innocuous content is devoid of political bias. The vast majority of student design projects deal with corporate needs, placing a heavy priority on the corporate economic sector of our society. Commerce is where we are investing time, budgets, skills and creativity. This is a decisive vote for economics over other potential concerns, including social, educational, cultural, spiritual and political needs. This is a political statement in itself, both in education and practice.

Art ignores the issues too

Postwar American art has greatly ignored the issues as well. The self-reference of abstract expressionism and minimalism has been largely divorced from external conditions. Pop art embraced materialism more than it critiqued it. The more recent Post-Modernist ironic parodies have been full of duplicity and offer no program as antidote to the appalling paradigms they deconstruct. Nevertheless recent years have brought a new involvement by artists in the social/political environment around them. A recent book, *The Reenchantment of Art,* advocates a second Post-Modernism, a reconstruction that moves beyond the detachment of Modernism and deconstruction. Suzi Gablik, the author, wants an end to the alientation of artists and aesthetics from social values in a new interrelational audience-oriented art.

There are signs that this is happening. Issue-oriented art has been spreading like wildfire among graduate students in the fine arts. At Cranbrook Academy of Art and a number of other design schools, fine arts students are attending our graphic design crits, eager to learn design methods for reaching their audiences. Fashion advertising is beginning to occasionally embrace issues – perhaps humanistic content is good for sales. Witness Esprit, Benetton, Moschino. That these clients are prepared to make social advocacy part of their message signals both a need and a new receptiveness in their audiences. Graphic design is a powerful tool, capable of informing, publicising, and propagandising social, environmental and political messages as well as commercial ones. But are many graphic designers prepared to deal with this type of content?

Undertaking the occasional piece of compassionate graphic design as a relief from business as usual is not the answer here. The choice of clients or content is crucial. The most fortunate can find a worthy cause in need of a designer with the funds to pay for professional design services. Unfortunately, good causes often seem to have the least resources in our present economic system. Is it possible to shape a practice around non-business clients or introduce social content into commercial work? The compassionate designer must plan an ethical practice strategically – and be an informed, involved citizen in a Jeffersonian participatory democracy, agile and flexible, prepared to turn the tools of visual communications to a broad spectrum of needs.

An end to detachment?

How does one educate graphic design students with an understanding of design as a social and political force? Can a political consciousness be trained? Can an educator teach values? The answer is probably no in the simplistic sense. However, the field of education has a well-developed area referred to as values clarification that offers many possibilities for graphic design educators. Too often we take individuals with 18 years of experience and strip them of their values, rather than cultivate those values for effective application in design practice.

In teaching, these issues must be raised from the beginning for the design student. This is not something to spring on the advanced student after their attitudes have been fixed on neutrality. At the core of this issue is the content of the projects we assign from the very first introductory exercise. Most introductory graphic design courses are based on abstract formal exercises inherited from the Bauhaus and the classic Basel school projects.

The detachment problem begins here. These projects either deal with completely abstract form – point, line and plane, for instance – or they remove imagery from context. The Basel graphic translation projects, so effective in training a keen formal sense, unfortunately use a process of abstractional analysis, thereby stripping imagery of its encoding symbolism. (I have to admit to being guilty of this in my assignments in past years.) Divorcing design form from content or context is a lesson in passivity, implying that graphic form is something separate and unrelated to subjective values or even ideas. The first principle is that all graphic projects must have content.

The type of content in each assignment is crucial. It is disheartening to see the vast number of undergraduate projects dedicated to selling goods and services in the marketplace devoid of any mission beyond business success. Undoubtedly all students need experience in this type of message and purpose. But cannot projects cover a broader mix of content, including issues beyond business? Cultural, social and political subjects make excellent communications challenges for student designers.

Project assignments can require content developed by the student which deals with public and personal social, political and economic issues and current events. The responsibility for developing content is a crucial one; it counteracts the passive design role in which one unquestioningly accepts client-dictated copy. On a practical level, we know how frequently all designers modify and improve client copywriting; many graphic designers

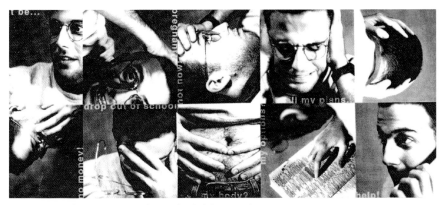

It Can't Be reproductive choice poster, by Cranbrook designer Sandra
Kelch: a role reversal personalises the dilemmas of an unwanted
pregnancy

become quite good writers and editors, so closely is our function allied to writing. In a larger sense, however, self-developed content and copy promotes two important attitudes in a design student.

One is the ability to develop personal content and subject matter, and an interest in personal design work, executed independently of client assignments. This method of working is much like that of fine artists who find their reward in a self-expression of personal issues. Secondly, the challenge to develop subject matter stimulates the design student to determine what matters on a personal level. A process of values clarification must go on in the student before a subject or attitude to that subject can be chosen. And the breadth of concerns chosen as subjects by fellow students exposes each student to a wider range of possibilities.

Clarification through critique
The critique process for issue-oriented work can be a very effective forum for values clarification. This is particularly true of group critiques in which all students are encouraged to participate, rather than the authoritarian

traditionalist crit in which the faculty staff do all the talking. In evaluating the success or failure of a piece of graphic communications, each critic must address the subject matter and understand the design student's stated intentions before weighing a piece's success. This expands the critique discussion beyond the usual and necessary topics of graphic method, form and technique. Tolerance as well as objectivity are required of each critique participant, in that they must accept and understand the student's intended message before evaluating the piece.

For instance, two fundamentalist Christian students recently brought their religiously oriented work to our Cranbrook graphic design crits for two semesters. It was a challenge – and a lesson in tolerance – for the other students to put aside their personal religious (or non-religious) convictions in order to give these students and their work a fair critique from a level playing field. It was quite remarkable – and refreshing – to find us all discussing spirituality as legitimate subject matter. This has held true for many other subjects from the universe of issues facing our culture today. These have included local and global environmental issues, animal rights, homelessness, feminism and reproductive choice.

The point here is content. As design educators, we cast projects almost as a scientist designs a laboratory experiment. The formula and the variables conspire to slant the results in one direction or another. The project assignment and the project critique are powerful tools that teach far more than explicit goals, and carry strong implicit messages about design and the role of designers.

Design history also offers a rich resource for understanding the relationship of form and content to socio-political contexts. We all know how often works from art and design history are venerated (and imitated) in an atmosphere which is divorced from their original context. By exploring the accompanying cultural/social/political histories, students can see the contextual interpendencies and make analogies to their own time.

Am I advocating the education of a generation of designers preoccupied with political activism, a kind of reborn 60s mentality? I think rather what I have in mind is nurturing a crop of active citizens, informed, concerned participants in society who happen to be graphic designers. We must stop inadvertently training our students to ignore their convictions and be passive economic servants. Instead we must help them to clarify their personal values and to give them the tools to recognise when it is appropriate to act on them. I do think this is possible. We still need objectivity, but this includes the objectivity to know when to invoke personal biases and when to set them aside.

Too often our graduates and their work emerge as charming manikins, voiceless mouthpieces for the messages of ventriloquist clients. Let us instead give designers their voices so they may participate and contribute more fully in the world around them.

Spain's new world

Jordi Montana SPAIN

Jordi Montana was born in Barcelona in 1949. His career has combined the role of Chief Executive of the DDI, the Spanish state agency for the development of industrial design, with teaching and consultancy on marketing and design management in both the public and private sectors. He has published several books about marketing and design, as well as many articles for the mainstream media.

The fashionable image of Spanish design is not just an exercise in style. Its high profile is underscored by substantial government collaboration in a programme which has helped small and medium-sized firms in Spanish industry to develop new products and find new markets.

Between 1982 and 1992, a wide variety of social agencies began paying a great deal of attention to design in Spain, among them the business community, the media and even the government. Multi-disciplinary design groups were formed and new designers emerged. Those designers who had been around for a while were looked up to as gurus. Design education, largely the province of private schools, showed a notable improvement. The state university system, which had previously overlooked design entirely, began offering graduate programs. Some of the business schools even jumped on the bandwagon, offering courses in design management.

Suddenly the market was flooded with design magazines and books for both a specialised audience and the general public. All the major newspapers began running design sections. Ordinary people started talking about design, designers – and of course Javier Mariscal. Design became a subject of heated discussion. Even the standard opening line for striking up conversation in a disco 'Do you work or study?', gave way to the joking inquiry: 'Do you study or just design?'

Design had become fashionable; so fashionable in fact that it found its way into politics. Even the government got involved in design. At the beginning of the 1980s the Catalan regional government commissioned and published an official report on design. The central government's Spanish Ministry of Industry put into practice a National Design Award. This is an award for product and graphic designers, and for companies whose products are noted for their design, which the King of Spain, personally, confers once every two years. The Ministry also drew up a Design Promotion Plan for the clothing industry which got underway in 1985 and has been periodically updated ever since.

Although reluctant at first to deal with people as bizarre as designers, businesses gradually began relying on them. Nowadays many of Spain's most competitive companies realise that product, package and graphic design, as applied to promotional material and corporate image, are essential to success in any market, especially since conditions now are vastly more difficult than they were ten years ago.

The truth is that this attention to design – to the process of inventing objects, forms and images, to the creative thought process, so easy to imagine and yet so difficult to carry out – has proved to be enormously beneficial. Companies that pay more attention and allocate more materials, time and human resources to designing their products, radically increase their chances of success.

Guilty parties in bad design

But if design is such a good thing, why are there so many badly designed products? Some models of steel teapots are unforgettable. The spout is designed for the liquid to go everywhere but in the cup. 'Shake before serving' it says on the Tetrapack. But if it is open, it will spill when you shake it. The situation is ridiculous.

I would say that there are three guilty parties here: businesses, designers and consumers in that order. There is, however, by extension, a fourth. This is government. As the Italians would say: *'Piove: governo ladro'* or 'it's raining and the government's to blame'. Businesses and any other institutions that commission designers deserve the largest share of the blame. This is because they don't invest as much as they should in design or because they invest it badly. Failure to invest might be due to the fact that they don't know any designers or they are not convinced that design is an advantage. It may also be because they are in such a hurry to get their products on to the market that they just don't have time. It often happens that companies dawdle over decisions to manufacture a new product and then, when the decision is made, they want to do everthing so fast that they make some serious mistakes.

Design can be a bad investment when the company and the designer are not on the same wavelength. This may be because no one bothered to specify the design requirements or because the design process was badly managed. Here designers have to share the blame. They have to realise that there is no such thing as industrial design without industry. They have to understand how the company works, but they don't have to take over the managing director's job. A little more business training, especially in marketing, would go a long way towards improving design.

Errors in planning, breakdowns in communication, lack of information and insufficient training are all basic causes of bad design, but they are not the only ones. Design users, in other words, the public in general, are also to blame. Knowledgeable and thinking consumers are demanding. These are consumers who are able to distinguish between products and choose the ones that work the best. They look for the safest, most efficient and durable products. They will demand products which are more ergonomic, more attractive, more original, more environmentally-friendly and easier to use. As such, they will be able to demand better design. The companies and designers who can respond to their demands will come out ahead. It's that simple. Or perhaps not quite.

Let's leave the fourth, and most guilty party, the government, until last and look now at the added problem of an uncertain and turbulent future. To put it as simply as possible, there are five issues that are going to affect design in the near future. These are new consumer habits, new kinds of production, new design technologies, new ecological requirements and new forms of cultural identity in design. This raises the issue of nationalism versus globalism.

The consumer of the 90s is a new kind of consumer. There are now population segments throughout the world whose consumer habits are similar because their lifestyles are similar. This is the result of an increasingly globalised network of communication. Today's consumers look for products with a higher symbolic content. Products now not only *are* something but, increasingly, *represent* something. Last but not least, more and more people are looking for quality rather than quantity.

Adapting to consumer tastes

New kinds of production aim to respond to the demands of these new consumers. Nowadays, factories have to adapt to consumer tastes and strive constantly to avoid massification. They have to act almost like individual craftsmen, producing custom-made products. Doing this means using new production technologies, new materials and new kinds of organisation, which in turn mean new kinds of design.

New design technologies are changing the entire design process from the initial sketch to the prototype. Among them are CAD, CAM and CAE (computer-aided design, manufacture and engineering) systems, rapid prototyping techniques, and new or improved design methods. These are often labelled with the latest buzzwords like re-engineering and benchmarking and are far removed from things like mechanical drawing and styrofoam models.

As the world becomes increasingly aware of the need for environmental protection, design will have to change and obey what can be called the law of the 3-Rs. This is: Reduce, Recycle, Retrieve. Reduce weight, volume and materials. Recycle and re-use components, which means using different materials and being more cautious and foresighted in terms of mixing components. Retrieve objects and parts. This involves thinking about a product's entire life cycle and not just its birth and coming of age as traditional design tends to do. From now on, we have to start thinking about how to lengthen the life cycle of our products. This means making them easier to maintain and repair and recycle after use.

We have a clash at present between designs that maintain a particular cultural identity and the more standardised designs that result from increasing globalisation. This raises a number of important questions. When and for what products should design be rooted in the local culture, regardless of whether or not it is exportable? When is rootless, neutral, functional design necessary or desirable? Will Scandinavian, Italian, or Spanish design as such continue to exist, if it actually ever did? Are Sony products an example of Japanese design? Is the design of McDonalds global design? Which is best? Now that times are tough and the future is filled with these seemingly unanswerable questions, what can governments do?

National Design Promotion Plan

Let me give an example. Towards the end of 1991 I worked with Spain's Ministry of Industry, Trade and Tourism drafting a National Design Promotion Plan. I was later asked to set up and head the DDI, the agency that would be in charge of putting the plan into operation. Our plan basically aims to make Spain's small and medium-sized businesses aware of the advantages of design and get them to invest more in design in order to improve their products. This is essentially done by providing advice and information which helps companies get in touch with designers. It is also done by improving design infrastructure by encouraging the use of new technologies, promoting designers' associations and fostering design promotion agencies. In addition, the DDI arranges training programmes for business people and designers, and organises campaigns to promote and publicise design.

In one year we helped small and medium-sized companies with over 300 different projects, almost 80 per cent of which involved product design for a wide variety of industries. For most of these companies, this was their first experience of working with a designer. All of them are small companies and some of them are located in parts of Spain where there is absolutely no design tradition.

The products may not be spectacular and probably none of them will ever win a design prize, but they have earned a place in the market and the companies that have produced them are moving forward along a new path. They have entered a new world with their new designs. For them this has definitely been the hour of a Design Renaissance.

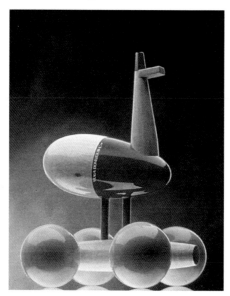

Wooden toy produced by Isaba, a small Spanish manufacturer of wooden playpens which was encouraged to diversify by DDI

A course for change

Daniel Weil ENGLAND

Daniel Weil is a partner in Pentagram, and Professor and Course Director of Industrial and Vehicle Design at London's Royal College of Art. He was educated in architecture in Argentina and studied industrial design at the RCA. Between 1985 and 1991 he produced products, furniture and interiors in partnership with Gerald Taylor for clients including Alessi, Knoll and Esprit.

Those familiar, linear problem-solving processes which created the industrial products of the past no longer apply in our post-electronic world. Academia has a searching role to play in nourishing a cultural and intellectual approach to complement technical skills in industrial design.

In preparing design students to face the future, I am certain of only two things. First, designers must have a point of view. Second, we will continue to change our minds. One of the things that the 1980s have shown us is that to be dogmatic, to assume that everything has already been done and learned, is out of step now. We are in for a time of change and we are *within* a time of change. It is my hope that we can hold onto this pluralism as long as the design profession exists.

The key to the future lies with the design process itself. The complexities of this process, which we have seen increased by the availability of information technology and the saturation of media and multi-media opportunities, indicate the need to embrace a multi-disciplinary approach to design. Design has become far more demanding than just the linear problem-solving process that we have enjoyed for so many years. In the next decade the familiar linear creative processes, rooted in the physical and representational world of mechanics and electronics, will limit our ability to respond to the more abstract complexities and overlaps generated by the increased use of computers and the so-called information explosion they bring.

The design process today is like an idea which has a kind of gravitational pull that attracts other ideas into orbit from many different realms, surrounding all of them with facts and information derived from a whole range of sources. The design decision could happen at any time, at any point along the orbital alignments of these ideas. So we arrive at a point where design is very relative with different conclusions for different people in different places. Therefore having a point of view is fundamental for designers, otherwise we will not have much to contribute, either as individuals or members of a team.

Challenges of a post-electronic world

The industrial design course at the Royal College of Art has a strategic part to play in the development of new creative processes and approaches – much needed in the profession – to meet and exploit the challenges of our post-electronic world. Industrial design must set about a re-interpretation of the language and values – 'the mindset' – of the mechanical and electronic world. This is not only because the new technologies demand the capacity for a broader and more abstract approach, but because of the emergence of such challenges to the established order as environmental awareness and major geo-political changes. This requires a reassessment of design, production and marketing throughout the industrial chain.

So we must also try to give more intellectual depth to the experience of designing. To meet all future challlenges, the profession must recapture its traditional cultural and strategic brief. A brief that requires the translation of cultural values into contemporary ideas and products. It will not be enough to provide competent technical or problem-solving services. As industries worldwide rethink their strategies, industrial designers must be able to respond and offer the vision and leadership that will shape the products of the twenty-first century.

Interpretation, representation and communication

On the course at the RCA we have therefore sought to help designers develop a 'point of view' and the strategy with which to implement it. In order to unravel the notion of strategy, we identified three fundamental issues: interpretation, representation and communication.

Through interpretation we develop the students' capacity to step back, analyse and deliver abstracts that suggest the possibilities within the cultural context of any project. Representation is central to the experience of the art school. Today we have people arriving with portfolios packed with amazing life drawings, but these clearly demonstrate that drawing has been taught to them as a craft, not as a method of thought. What they have learned as a method of thought is sketching, but what they have never discovered is how to put these two elements of drawing together.

Design education has never benefited from the developments, both in interpretation and representation, in twentieth century art. This is amazing when you consider that design is a thoroughly modern experience. So while we would like students to retain the skill, the craft of drawing, we introduce them to the idea of thinking while drawing in order to benefit from everything from Cubism to conceptual art. We enrich the visual language used by our students to explore and communicate ideas in a more imaginative, flexible and expressive way.

Communication is obviously central to all aspects of the design process. We develop students' ability to communicate, to link and express the relationships between their ideas and form, function, marketing and the many other commercial and cultural factors which make up today's complex projects. We constantly experiment with and test new approaches in resolving such projects.

Finding new methods of communication has been badly hampered, particularly in the design fields, because for some decades now designers have communicated between themselves in the same way that they have communicated to their clients. This is where I feel we should follow the example of architecture which seems to have been much more able to escape the dogmatic approach. Architects are used to drawing in many different ways: they develop a language to suit the project and their ideas.

By actually drawing and representing to our fellow designers in the same way we represent to clients, we somehow reduce all the possibilities of interpretation. We eliminate the excitement and the possibility of triggering ideas in others. We have worked very hard with our students to reinvent the ways in which we communicate and present work to each other.

A duty to teach leadership

At the RCA, we benefit from having only post-graduate students, which means that they arrive with the traditional skills of technical ability and high standards of creative ability. However, we have identified the need to teach designers in a slightly different way to give them the opportunity to develop and manage the design process. I think it is the duty of education, and the duty of the design profession, to ensure that young designers get the advantage now of the experience that we as professionals achieved only after ten years of practice. We must make the complex process of designing easier.

Perhaps most fundamentally, we have a duty to teach leadership. Industrial design has probably the longest design process of all in the design profession. We have a duty to try to understand all the contexts for design because if we intend to be involved from the very beginning to the very end of a project, we must know when to call upon the expertise available in graphic design or fashion design or any of the other design disciplines, as part of the multi-disciplinary experience.

Through the teaching of these fundamentals, we encourage students to develop maturity and authority to weigh and establish a hierarchical importance of ideas, process and events to enable them to become design innovators in a strategic capacity.

Relationship between objects and culture

In order to achieve this understanding, we run a series of projects which examine the relationship of industrial design to both industry and society. We aim to foster an earlier and more proactive role in product development and an attitude amongst our designers which is proactive and therefore able to perceive and exploit the opportunities offered by both technological and social change. Our aim is to renew the profession's commitment to the cultural objectives of design in the development of products of integrity and real value.

To develop an understanding of the relationship between objects and culture, our first project in the course is based around objects that are fairly simple technologically, and which have a long tradition and history, so there is no way you can avoid the cultural issues behind them. For example, in 1991 the project set was a clock for our time and the clocks designed by the students were objects which addressed more than the simple action of telling the time. They became indicators of our social and cultural experience.

Museum mask designed by Dominic Jones, Industrial Design, RCA: a magnifying glass incorporated in the mask increases awareness of detail

Comedia del Arte mobile dining trolley, by RCA designers David Elliot and Stefan Reichl: hospitality as theatre

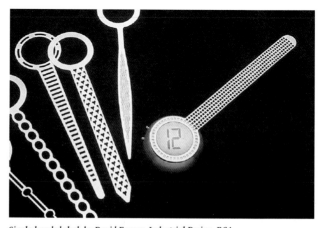

Single-handed clock by David Farage, Industrial Design, RCA

Working with Alessi

We have been involved in projects with Alessi for two years now. One of the major problems which we face today when new forms and new ideas enter our culture is how to explain them. The Alessi brief calls for an understanding, on many levels, of the object and its cultural role. It demands an attitude which extends to considering how the object is made, aiming for manufacturing simplicity without cultural devaluation. A project of this kind has an extraordinary effect upon students. It provides an entirely different type of motivation. This produces innovative ideas which embody technical excellence and creative invention, and which set standards for the future of industrial design education and practice.

All project work highlights one of the important themes on the RCA course: this is the value of group activity. It is the group that sets the standard for the individual. It is understood from the beginning that, because of the complexity we face today, nobody as an individual can match the results the group can achieve. Therefore all students try to match the group standards through individual effort.

Academic role as a testing ground

The relationship between the profession and education is central to the success of industrial design. It is for education to explore and experiment in order to provide the research, data and approaches that will enable practitioners to respond to the opportunities offered by the new technologies, ideas and global alignments. In order to create a useful dialogue and partnership between the professional and academic fields, education must use the freedom and the energy afforded by the academic world. We must aim to equip our students with the intellectual approaches necessary to complement their technical skills. In this period of change and challenge, it is vital that education should re-establish its place as a testing ground and as a laboratory for the trial of new perspectives and approaches that the day-to-day pressures prevent practitioners from attempting.

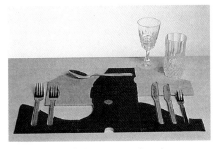 

Etiquette by RCA designers Sam Hecht and Wayne James: a template to set the table according to the rules of etiquette. The presentation box opens out to become the place setting

123

Section 4:
Products of tomorrow

The essays in this section explore the future of product development against a background of escalating technological and social change. New technologies don't always mean progress, as reflected by **Bill Moggridge** in his analysis of the ironies that underscore our love of new artefacts, and **Gillian Crampton Smith** in her call for radical improvements in the design of the human interface in electronic products. Ingrained social attitudes are a problem too, as **Roger Coleman** argues in his essay on the product design implications of an ageing population. Why do we insist on treating design for older people as design for the disabled or infirm? Why not design for everyone – universal design? Indeed, despite the current problems of untamed technology and outdated cultural stereotypes, **James Woudhuysen** warns against a retreat from universalism, rationalism and humanism – the three major gains of the Renaissance and of the Enlightenment. The section ends, however, with **Sir Terence Conran's** view that the future for designers lies not in mass markets but in niche areas where skill and imagination are more highly prized.

In defence of the Enlightenment

James Woudhuysen ENGLAND

James Woudhuysen is Associate Director in the Social Futures Unit at the Henley Centre for Forecasting, Britain's best known 'think-tank' on the future of economic and social behaviour. He has worked on corporate strategy for UK cities including Birmingham, Manchester and Glasgow, for companies including Compaq, IBM, Midland Bank, London Transport, Philips and Unisys, and the governments of Canada, France and Norway. Woudhuysen has written for publications including the *Financial Times*, the *Economist* and *Management Today*.

Three of the major breakthroughs of the Renaissance and of the Enlightenment – rationalism, humanism and universalism – are under threat from dark and pessimistic forces in society today. To develop progressive products and lifestyles of the future, these forces must be resisted.

We could talk about the technologies of the future – about micro-mechanics, biometrics, mobile telephony. We could discuss multi-media and how old people are going to cope. We could investigate developments in high definition TV or computer-supported collaborative work. We could expose the bogus green claims of manufacturers, or analyse the crisis of the premium brand. All these issues are important, but I want to go straight to the core theme of the conference. I want to defend the Renaissance, as well as the Enlightenment, because we live in a time when many people want to overturn the gains those two eras bought us.

The Renaissance of the sixteenth century was a period of republican city states and of increasing criticism of the church. There was a great amount of admiration and respect for nature; but at the same time, there was a growing respect not just for landscape or animals, but for human beings.

One of the great insights of the Renaissance was made by the British poet, Sir Philip Sidney, in his *Defence of Poetry*. In that work, he said 'Nature never set forth the Earth in so much tapestry as diverse poets have done; neither with so pleasant rivers, fruitful trees, sweet-smelling flowers, nor whatsoever else may make the too-much-loved Earth more lovely. Her world is brazen; the poets only deliver a golden.' [1]

Nature's world is brazen, but the creativity and thought and action and planning of poets, of human beings, is what distinguishes us from nature. A bee may work in a hive, an otter may build a dam, but they don't design things in the kind of conscious, articulated way that mankind does.

This leads to my first premise. A fundamental rethinking for design may be necessary, in that products related to work will be more important than products related to consumption. It is in that sense that we can say that the act of creativity, of work, is what is human about us. The act of consumption, by contrast, is something that we share with animals. Animals eat, animals excrete, but we're above that. We're creative, we are designers and we make progress in design. And that fundamental distinction between work and consumption will become more apparent to us as we all find work a more gruelling business in the 1990s. It also leads me to the Enlightenment.

Three Enlightenment breakthroughs

What were the gains of the Enlightenment? First, there was rationalism – the idea that there was a reason for things. Second, there was humanism, summed up by Pope in his *Essay on Man:* 'Know then thyself, presume not God to scan / The proper study of Mankind is Man'.[2] Finally, the Enlightenment taught us universalism – for example, the doctrine that all people were in some way equal.

It was Adam Smith, a Scot, who most clearly represented the Enlightenment in Britain. Smith applied rational theory to the actions and the work of human beings, and, in his celebrated analysis of the 17 operations that went on to make a pin, developed the idea of a division of labour.[3] Smith also developed the ideas of value and of price in products.

Why was all this important? Because when we come to 1798, little more than 20 years after Smith published his *magnum opus,* an English parson by the name of the Reverend Thomas Robert Malthus made a retrograde step, against the spirit of the Enlightenment.[4] What Malthus concentrated on was consumption. He said that there were too many mouths to feed, given the natural resources available on the land. He wasn't interested in the quality of human beings and the special quality their work has of making things with a market value and a price.

Malthus suggested that there were too many dissolute working class people consuming and also breeding too much. For him, the only proper kind of consumption was the consumption of the aristocracy and of the church – in the person of the Reverend Thomas Robert Malthus and people like him. The whole emphasis of Malthus was on the burdensome *quantity* of the poor.

Beyond the 1980s

The Renaissance and the Enlightenment were actually rather relevant to the period which has recently ended – the 1980s. What Ronald Reagan and Margaret Thatcher said, and I'm afraid some people still say it, is that one human being's experience can never be commensurate with another's. As Margaret Thatcher put it, 'There is no such thing as society. There are only individuals and their families.'

Like Malthus, this represented a step backwards from the Enlightenment. But after an era of unbridled individualism, today less is once again more in design. Instead, therefore, of market segmentation, it is a moment now for changed priorities. Our three Enlightenment breakthroughs now need defending as principles. That way, we can go forward in the aggressive and politicised manner that Stefano Marzano recommends to us, earlier in this book. Let me explore those principles in a little more depth.

Rationalism must be the foundation of the design of the world of products and lifestyles of tomorrow. Rationalism also means that we must have a critical attitude to today's fashionable theories. Take, for example, Chaos Theory – the idea that you can't explain anything because life is so chaotic. As Spielberg's movie *Jurassic Park* repeats it, a butterfly need only flap its wings in South America and something happens as a consequence in Glasgow. In this perpsective, the natural must take primacy over the social, and we will never be able to understand the world.

This kind of anti-rational theory is growing in influence. After all, the media have recently rediscovered our old friend, Evil. Now as it happens, one of the doctrines of the Enlightenment was that evil didn't really exist. Yet there are many people today who will brand races and individuals as thoroughly evil without trying to explain them by any rational means.

Against all this, I want to propose *la douche froide de Descartes* – the cold shower of Cartesian logic. And I want to say this because in the past few years pessimism about the future, and in particular pessimism about technology, has grown quite fast. We read sinister novels like William Gibson's *Neuromancer.* My kids are dying to see the murderous nature of *Robocop.* We read magazines like *Mean Sega Machines,* which says that it wants to prepare us for 'the final fight'. It is looking gloomy out there – yet in fact there is no need to be gloomy at all.

It is not that technology doesn't create problems; of course it does. But if we believe in the primacy of humanity and mankind, then we believe that we have the capacity still to solve those problems. I now want to indicate just two technologies that pose some of these questions very poignantly.

New materials and transport

Ezio Manzini has managed to bring to us much of the magic, the possibilities and the potential of materials.[5] Today, we should celebrate refractory ceramics, lights made of leather and zips, lights which can crawl up poles of conductive Velcro. This is the kind of progress that we need in the 1990s, a progress which is unashamedly in favour of a considered and rational approach to technology, one which looks forward to roomtemperature super conductors and even now can make Badedas bottle-tops in a pleasurably exotic kind of plastic.

Plastics can reduce weight in cars and aeroplanes. They bring ecological problems, but they also save fuel. We have to be steadfast in our appreciation that technology is not a villain – it is just what we make it.

The high speed train and the electric car illustrate similar principles. From Amtrak in America to the Shinkansen in Japan, the high speed train raises some charged issues. In about 20 years time, if British Rail will allow me, I will be able to get on at Waterloo and travel to Paris in an hour or two. But if Paris becomes a suburb of London, the effect will be that people are going to be crammed together more. Not only will the high speed train appear to turn Europe into one large city, it will in the process appear to increase population density. Do we then want the high speed train or don't we?

I submit that we do want it. I submit that there's nothing wrong with more people being put together. By the same token, I think we have to come out in favour of the electric car. The infrastructural problems with electric cars are enormous. Everybody knows that to make batteries and to charge them from power stations generates a lot of pollution. But at least an electric car will not put fumes in your face. Are we in favour of that? Yes. Do we think technology can solve today's very grave green problems? I think we have to say yes.

Humanism, ethics and the Third World

How do we achieve what Doris Lessing has described – and Michael Wolff has echoed – as the 'substance of "we" feeling'? If you read Paul Kennedy's new book *Preparing for the Twentieth Century,* you will find that the big problem facing the world is our old Malthusian friend, over-population – not in Britain, as Malthus had it, but overpopulation in the Third World. [6] This dogma is the contemporary shape of anti-humanism.

The old divisions are still there, but they take a new form. Indeed the Malthusian argument has now got a green twist. It is said that because there are too many people in the Third World, they will add to the Greenhouse effect. Too many breeders, too many breathers: so just go home and get some contraception, otherwise you're screwing up my personal atmosphere.

One can laugh, but there is a need to mount a very strong counter-argument. In our profession, if ethics are important, we have to make the point that the problem is not over-population in the Third World. The problem is under-design. The reason that the world lacks water is not because there isn't enough water on the planet – two thirds of the planet's surface is covered by water – but that we don't have the irrigation systems; we're not prepared to make that a priority. We are not prepared to put human beings at the centre of things.

Before we rush to castigate the Third World for having too many people and too many ethnic hatreds, and before we also rush to 'respect' its 'culture', its charming raffia work and all that, I say, unpopularly, that we should think twice. I say that we have to use the most advanced technology and design to cure these problems, which are not to do with the backwardness and stupidity of the Third World, but to do with social conditions, to do with human beings.

The problems can be solved, because all the degradation that characterises Third World cities is man-made. These cities weren't naturally vile; we made them, so we have to unmake them. We can unmake them with German solar power or with American bloodtesting systems. This is the way to the 'all-win' global economic strategies that Erskine Childers so persuasively calls for in section 1 of this book.

A universalist synthesis

The third principle of the Enlightenment was universalism. The point I want to make here is how much we need to draw from people whose experience is very different to ours, and how everyone can benefit from that experience. We really do have to take a lesson from the East. In this regard, please note that shoes from Taiwan are being designed not just with springs, but with air conditioning in them.

We have so much to learn from the Taiwanese and from the Chinese. Even NASA, in its plan for a $12bn space station, will have to shack up with Russia's MIR. In Japan, too, they have given the world ski-lifts complete with hot-tubs and *sake* to drink. I'm not sure that this is necessarily the solution to all our problems, but it certainly belies many of our stereotypes of the Japanese.

What we mean by universalism is upholding the best design achievements, not of our own nation, but of every other nation around the world: upholding them, mastering them, synthesising them into products for all countries and all walks of life.

The issue is not about being politically correct and saying 'I respect your culture'. It is about universal access to design. It is thus about democratic rights – a concept that was pioneered by the Enlightenment, but which today is often under threat. We have to resist that threat if we're to live up to our responsibilities as designers.

In this context, we need to speak out in favour of what IT people call adaptive interfaces: interfaces that recognise who you are, learn about you, and adjust themselves to match. Above all, we need to advocate adaptive interfaces that understand the power and the subtlety of human speech. Voice-operated software is the last great frontier if we're to make access and democracy part of our design movement.

I love pen computers. But in the Third World, 90 per cent of the population cannot write. Even in America, about half the population is supposed to be functionally illiterate. Voice recognition can solve these problems. Many other problems could be solved by machine translation, on which the Japanese are working. These things have to be technological, social, economic, financial and design priorities of the future.

Please note that the universalism advocated here does not deny the specificity of particular individuals or locations. On the contrary: it is only by understanding what is common to all people, countries or cities that the idiosyncrasies of each can be set in sharp relief. Core designs can be modified to accommodate these idiosyncrasies but the problem is first to arrive at those core designs.

Universalism in practice: the idea of modes

How can we apply all this in practice? Conventional marketing theory wants to divide us all into As and Bs and C1s and C2s. If it is really sophisticated, it will go on about lifestyles. Briefly, here is a method by which you can make your products more accessible to people, more humanistic and more universal.

Every day, you and I go through phases of feeling like an A (upper middle class), a B (middle class) a D (unskilled) and an E (unemployed). When we're running for a plane we feel over 80, even if we're 40. So we can see that conventional market segmentation has its merits, but that very often, in our attitudes and behaviour, we elude its categories.

If, by contrast, we focus on what we at the Henley Centre call 'modes', that can be much more productive. A mode usually appears around an occasion of use. When you go to an airport, you can be in panic mode. You can be in 'first time at Heathrow' mode. What we need to understand is the number of all these different modes, the nature of them, the relative priority of them, and so on. Then we can prepare the products and systems and graphic interfaces to match.

UK POPULATION % OWNING

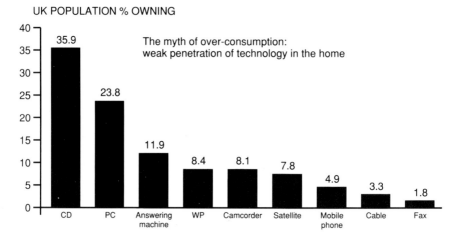

Source: The Henley Centre Planning for Social Change 1992

Keynes and consumption

To emerge from a period of crisis and move toward the kind of rational, humanistic, universal and comprehensive perspective that is needed, we need a new theory of design and of society. We will get that theory, but it will not be the old theory of John Maynard Keynes.

If you read the preface to the German edition of Keynes' *The General Theory of Money, Interest and Employment,* you will find a very interesting remark. There, in 1936, Keynes had the nerve to make the point that his theory was more applicable to totalitarian societies than to democratic ones. So state intervention, the policy of Keynes, doesn't look like a very attractive solution to our problems. We know that monetarism and Post-Modernism, the ideas of the 1980s, are not a solution, but nor are state intervention and Modernism. That is why we need a new theory.

The final thing to remember about Keynes is that his focus, like Malthus, was all on how to increase consumption to combat lack of effective demand. Now, of course, we find our modern-day Keynesians inverting his doctrine, and in a green manner, saying that we all need to cut consumption.

This in itself is very ironic. Precisely at a time when you and me *are* cutting consumption – that's what we're forced to do in a recession – our green friends tell us to make still more cuts. You can't get a glass of water in California without them asking you whether you really need it. Thus California's water shortage is turned from a social problem to do with dams and pipe design to a natural, individual and moral one. In the same way, we're all now supposed to feel guilty when we get in a car. So let's be careful before we rush into Keynes and consumption as the basis of our new theory.

Guarding against nostalgia and false universalism

Through the better design of work, we can achieve that difficult and untrendy thing, progress. By the same token, we need to guard against nostalgic retro-design. Do we really want a design culture which is like the rock music charts right now, where nearly everything comes from 30 years ago?

Let me urge you, too, to guard against *false* universalism. The universalism of Vodaphone, whose graphics say, in Russian Constructivist style, that everybody must have a mobile phone, but which also insists that everybody must wave a Union Jack about it at the same time. The universalism of Rupert Murdoch who is so politically correct nowadays that he insists that you and me, in an ecstatic state of empowerment, determine the future of electronic media, not media barons like him. And let's also watch out for the bogus universalism of the United Nations, whose little plastic spacemen came out of my Sugar Puffs packets in the 1960s, but who, in their blue helmets, look pretty much like spacemen to people in Somalia right now.

The stakes today are very high in design. The forces which want to send us back to times before the Renaissance and the Enlightenment are growing. We can go back or we can go forward. I suggest we go forward. I suggest that we become representatives and partisans of the future. To professionalise ourselves, to read widely, to understand and really uphold the examples of other countries, is tough for us to do – but that is the only way out of the present impasse.

During the Renaissance, the philosopher Francis Bacon wrote an essay called *Of Superstition*.[7] I believe that something it said really applies to our Malthusian friends, and to all the dark, irrational theories I have mentioned. Bacon wrote that the causes of superstition had a lot to do with what he called 'barbarous times, especially joined with calamities and disasters'.

Let's stand out against the forces of superstition in the 1990s.

References

1. Quoted in David Norbrook, 'Introduction', in D Norbrook and HR Woudhuysen, *The Penguin Book of Renaissance Verse 1509-1659* (Penguin 1992)
2. Pope, *Essay on Man*, Epistle 11
3. See Adam Smith, *The Wealth of Nations* 1776 (Pelican 1970)
4. See Malthus, *An Essay on the Principles of Population as it Affects the Future Improvement of Society*, 1798
5. See Ezio Manzini's *The Material of Invention* 1986 (The Design Council 1989), and Manzini's *Artefatti: verso una nuova ecologia dell'ambiente atificiale in Domus* 1990
6. Kennedy P, *Preparing for the Twentieth Century* (Harper Collins 1993)
7. Bacon, *Essays Civil and Moral*, 1625 (Cassell 1889)

The Oldie logo: a designer's view of old age

Age: the challenge for design

Roger Coleman ENGLAND

Roger Coleman is Senior Research Fellow and Director of the Design Age programme at London's Royal College of Art. Design Age is an action-research programme exploring the implications for design of the ageing of First World populations. Coleman has a special interest in user and environment-friendly design and has lectured widely on the subject.

First World populations are living longer. The over-50s have growing economic power. Yet stereotypical views of age confuse design for an ageing population with design for disability and special needs. New product strategies are needed to produce better solutions for people of all ages.

Mick Jagger recently turned 50 and Roger Daltrey of The Who did not die, as the song suggested, before he got old. This is a fact that their generation – my generation – has to come to terms with now. In the 1960s we simply did not consider the possibility of being old one day. The reasons for this could lie in the fact that until as recently as 1950 the probability of our surviving to enjoy any significant period of retirement was low. Consequently there was no advantage in anticipating a lengthy 'old age'. After 1950, however, things began to change and now four out of every ten adults is over 50. My generation and those who follow now have to confront longevity. Time has caught up with us.

My earlier understanding of age reflected my parents' idea that it was a relatively short period of slippers-by-the-fire, of the bent back and walking stick of the road sign used by *The Oldie* magazine in its logo. (Incidentally the road sign is a designer's view of age, not an old person's.) Age was something akin to a rainy day that one saved up against, and the dominant view of age is still framed in such pre-war terms. That is why, when most designers talk about design and older people, they assume that means designing for people with disabilities or special needs. That is why, when the caring professions talk about 'the elderly', they can do so in ways that suggest all old people are dependent and living in institutions when more that 95 per cent of over-50s live at home; and when gerontologists talk about old people, their professional or academic objectivity can reinforce a them-and-us view which makes it difficult to acknowledge that old people are simply ourselves in the future.

Too many people carry that road sign around in their heads. It is what they think of when they think 'old', and it brings with it a patronising and complacent mythology which is utterly inappropriate to a world in which the old are rapidly outnumbering the young. What we need instead are new models of age; models of independent, active life (physical, mental and economic); models that acknowledge the diversity and talents of our ageing population; models that liberate rather than restrict. Above all, we need models that recognise our adult potential as active and contributing to society for a period extending across 60 or more years

This is a great challenge to us all, and design has a vital role to play here as enabler, shaping a world that is user-friendly, flexible and accommodating, that adjusts to our changing capabilities as we age, and offers us a chance to adapt by remaining active and fit for as long as possible. This challenge was taken up by the Royal College of Art when, with the support of the Helen Hamlyn Foundation and Safeway plc, it launched an action-research programme exploring the implications for design and communication of the ageing of populations across the First World. I am privileged to lead the Design Age programme at the RCA: age is perhaps *the* design challenge of the future.

Design which reinforces stereotypes

As a judge of the New Design for Old section of the RSA Student Design Awards in Britain, I see a high proportion of entries each year falling into the gadget category – gadgets for opening doors, gadgets for opening jars, add-ons and adaptations. These aids, often ingenious, address the fact that many everyday objects make life difficult for anyone who is less than able-bodied. But they still inevitably stigmatise the user and they reinforce the 'old equals infirm' stereotype. What I don't see enough of are things I can't wait to own, and what I am all too aware of is that so many things need redesigning and rethinking if they are to work well for people of all ages.

It is my belief that if we design with the needs of older people, of ourselves in the future, in mind at every step of the process then we will arrive at products which work better for everybody, regardless of age or ability. And it is important to remember that when it comes to infrastructure – buildings, roads, stations, rolling stock and so on – we are talking about things which may last as long as we do: if we design these things for ourselves at age 30 we may find that they do not work for us at 70. This is an important point, because older people are not a different species; they are quite simply ourselves in the future.

But what point is there in thinking in this way if we can only see the negative side of age, if we can only see it as something to be avoided and postponed? My answer is that this view of age is so dominant because, like the road sign, it was framed in the past. Today's reality is very different. At the end of the nineteenth century the majority of the UK population was aged under 30, and the proportion surviving to 70 tiny. Then it would have been unreasonable to anticipate anything other than a short retirement: a period of rest after a lifetime of work. One hundred years later, things are very different. Life expectation has increased by 50 per cent during this century. Four out of ten British voters are already over 50, and by 2021 the over 50s are likely to hold a majority.

The process we are involved in constitutes a radical and probably irreversible shift away from youth-dominated societies. Understanding it will involve a complete rethink of what age means, and as we undertake that, we will be forced to draw a new map of life in which the 30 or more years we can look forward to after the age of 50 will be as important to us as the 30 years before.

In many senses 50 can now be regarded as the centre of gravity of our adult lives. If we are to enjoy the new lease of life that implies, we will need to see enormous changes in the design of everyday objects and environments. That in itself is a considerable challenge to design, but I believe the bigger and really exciting challenge is to begin to conceive of a world that is radically different and infinitely more user-friendly than the world we inhabit at the moment. New technology offers us the ability to make big changes, but the uses we make of it will be shaped by how we see ourselves in the future.

Drive of the marketplace

Of course, it would be naive to suggest that the sort of changes I have suggested will come about without the commercial drive of the marketplace. According to Danielle Barr, director of Third Age Marketing, people over 50 have more disposable income than any other population group. The economic power of this group is quite formidable: they account for 30 per cent of all consumer expenditure – over £30 billion – and account for 60 per cent of all savings. Yet there is very little evidence of this economic power in the marketplace because this group are ignored by marketing.

Consequently, says Barr, they are becoming angry and frustrated by the irony that even though they have the time and the money to spend, there are not many things that appeal to them. Many more products and designs actually *irritate* them because they are so poorly designed ergonomically. Danielle Barr suggests a reason for the slowness to change: marketing departments, advertising agencies and design consultancies are, on the whole, staffed by young people. The average age of a brand manager is 29. Agency creative teams are often even younger.

Shifting from margin to mainstream

Nine months in 1988 saw the confirmation of the ozone hole, the publication of the *Green Consumer Guide*, Mrs Thatcher's pro-environment speech, and an intensive media campaign orchestrated by a relatively small group of committed individuals and organisations. By the end of that year, environmentalism was here to stay and most major companies now regard environment as a competitive factor. That dramatic shift from margin to mainstream took the design community, and in particular design education, by surprise. So, as age moves onto the mainstream agenda, I think it is vitally important that we in the design community are prepared and up to speed.

The first step is to recognise that this is a new and uncharted area. Just as older people lack positive role models, we are also lacking in examples of age-friendly design – although pioneers like Maria Benkzton of Egonomi Design Gruppen in Sweden have worked for 20 years on user-friendly design for disability which provides solutions that work better for people of all ages.

Developing an understanding of older users, in the sense of well-researched ergonomics, is clearly one key to a user-friendly future. Another is understanding the needs and aspirations of older people, and one way of doing this is to try and see the world 'through other eyes'. Age Concern England is now running courses in which participants can begin to find out what it feels like to be older. The programme originated in Canada and has proved very successful in helping decision-makers appreciate how they can improve the provision they make for older customers.

Innovation most often comes about when we change our viewpoint and look at things anew. The changing age-profile of First World nations allows us a unique opportunity to question the way we have designed in the past, and to approach the future from a different perspective. In doing this we are all treading new ground and so are unlikely to get everything right, but it is very important that we explore the widest range of options in the most imaginative way. If we don't, then we can all look forward to an extended and very dull old age.

Paradoxes of the future
Bill Moggridge

Bill Moggridge is responsible for formulating strategic directions for IDEO Product Development. He founded Moggridge Associates in 1969, building a product development consultancy with clients in most European countries, the USA, Korea, Taiwan and Japan. IDEO, formed in 1991 by Moggridge Associates, David Kelley Design and Matrix Product Design, has clients including NEC, Ford, Xerox, Hoover, Apple, Philips and Moulinex. The company pioneered a multi-disciplinary approach to product development combining industrial design with engineering, and interaction design with human factors.

As new technologies reshape our patterns of living and working, the onslaught of change is highlighting a series of ironies. How can we equate our love of leisure products with a concern for the environment? And why, in an age of software, are so many products still so hard to use?

The future seems to be coming at us faster all the time. In order to create products that will be right for their time, we need to have ideas about the direction of this onslaught of change. Here are five notions about the changes that will affect the design of products and the lifestyles of the people who will use them.
- Companies are going virtual, but still have shareholders.
- Technologies are going soft, but are still hard to use.
- Information is moving, but we are staying put.
- We are taking more time off, but can we find time to turn green?
- Virtual reality is elusive, but video is toasting.

Companies are going virtual, but still have shareholders
A recent *Business Week* article featured the concept of the Virtual Corporation. It points out that an increasing number of new products are being developed by teams put together as temporary alliances between more than one company, often aggressively competitive with each other in their normal activities. For example, IBM has teamed up with Apple to form a new product development company called Talligent, and the Newton series of pen-driven computers was developed by Apple and Sharp.

It seems that almost every day a new alliance of surprising bedfellows is announced as cable and satellite communications converge with computers in the exploding world of multimedia, interactive entertainment and services; witness, for example, TV Interactive Theater, brought to you by Microsoft (the world's largest software company), Intel (the biggest microprocessor chip-maker), and Jerrold-General Instruments (one of the two largest cable TV hardware manufacturers).

One wonders how the shareholders of each individual company can keep track of what is happening, and who can be held responsible for success and failure. The renaissance of design in this context will have to be flexible and innovative in international and cross-cultural relationships, both from company to company and from country to country.

Technologies are going soft, but are still hard to use

Steve Job's Next Computer has been forced to stop manufacturing products, becoming a solely software company. Microsoft has emerged as the dominant computer company in America, while IBM struggles to maintain viability; what a contrast to the brightness of Big Blue a decade ago. The leaders of both computer and consumer electronics companies are converting their businesses to software as fast as they can restructure their R&D resources, as three-dimensional product development flows eastwards to the Asian Tigers. Is the Design Renaissance ready to create software?

Digital watches are still hard to use. When they were first created there was an excuse to design the controls for the simplest and most economical hardware and software programming, but by now it is surprising that the set-up controls are still kind to chips but cruel to users. As more and more products include electronics, the challenge of interaction design looms larger.

There are a growing number of practitioners around now, but education lags behind, with some fledgling courses around the world, but only the CRD (Computer Related Design) course at the Royal College of Art in London producing fully competent interaction designers. It is significant that more than half the students graduating in 1993 were snapped up by Microsoft and Apple.

Information is moving, but we are staying put

Digital information can be communicated by many means that would have destroyed the integrity of the previous analog generation. Data highways are being installed for business; satellite communications and cable networks are reaching lots of homes; digital cellular services are being announced, so that people will soon be able to transmit information to wearable phones and portable computers without cables.

I spend enough time on planes to look forward with intense anticipation to the change in lifestyle that improvements in the movement of information will permit. I spent the first years of my career living and working in the same building, and look forward to doing so again in the latter years. A key idea in IDEO's Greenhouse Project with NEC is 'from office to home'. This is helping us to think about how to design computers that belong in a domestic environment, with an appearance that is sympathetic in a living room, and with features for space saving and storage.

We are taking more time off, but can we find time to turn green?

Those of us who are lucky enough to be gainfully employed are finding more time for leisure, yielding lots of opportunities to design products for relaxation and sport. A design revolution has already happened with products such as athletic shoes, ski equipment, wind surfers, roller blades and bicycles, and we can expect that there are more to come.

The almost flippant nature of these products for *time off* is in stark contrast to the deeply felt concern about environmental issues. Product designers live on the bubbly surface of secondary industry, synthesising solutions from materials and energy that have been produced at deeper levels of primary industrial production, where the most significant efforts to turn green will need to be made.

There are things that we can do to make a difference however, for example with design for disassembly and choosing materials for recycling, or trying to make sure that we specify materials that have been created with a minimum of damage to the environment. At IDEO we have appointed green experts, so that our designers know who to ask when a choice arises. We also publish and update a checklist to remind ourselves of the most effective contribution that we can make.

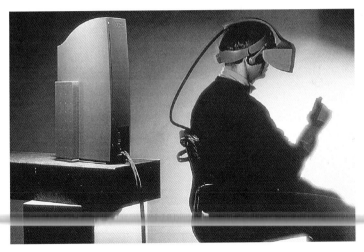

Virtual reality system from VPL, with glove controller and 3D colour headset. Industrial design by IDEO

Virtual reality is elusive, but video is toasting

Most people identify virtual reality with the mask and data glove made famous by Jaron Lanier of VPL. The idea of wearing a computer is in itself engaging. You can easily imagine putting on clothes which allow you to enter a different world, and be seduced by flights of fancy.

Virtual reality has been around for long enough now for us to ask if the obvious applications for the technology have a value which is greater than entertainment. Does the manipulation of the parameters in the kitchen help the user to design a better place to cook in? Larson's cartoon of a dog using a fear meter to test for the difference between a guest and an intruder offers an apt reminder that our real senses may offer us greater sensitivity than artificial ones. The value of visual reality may be elusive, but most of us will probably be content to remain substantive rather than virtual.

There are more than six million video camcorders in use in the USA alone. This is the ubiquitous medium of our time, and a video editing revolution is upon us, comparable to the impact of desktop publishing on print. Professional video editing equipment costs something close to £100,000 so that very few people have had access to editing in the past.

A video toaster can now be bought for something close to £5,000 complete with effects like wipes, fades, page turns and zooms, together with title graphics and animations. The video toaster consists of a personal computer, a box of electronics and a tape deck, and will allow a hoard of low-overhead editors to feed the hungry cable and satellite channels. The video toaster is aimed at a commercial market, but there are other desk-top editing systems more suitable for artistic endeavour, on which programmes such as Zype are being produced.

The future holds a potential design renaissance in multi media, with video as the key.

Humanising technology: could do better

Gillian Crampton Smith ENGLAND

Gillian Crampton Smith is Professor of Computer Related Design at London's Royal College of Art. She has previously been responsible for design and art direction on various publications including *Architecture Today*, the *Times Literary Supplement* and *The Sunday Times*. She has acted as a consultant to Apple Computer Advanced Technology Group, Stanford University, and the National Gallery, London, specialising in human/computer interaction. She lectures internationally on various aspects of design and computing.

Most of the new electronic products and systems of the Information Age have interfaces designed from the point of view of manufacturer efficiency, not user convenience. To improve interaction and create richer user 'narratives', designers must not sit on the sidelines and leave it all to the engineers.

We don't really know how the Information Age is going to pan out. All we can guess is that it is going to be very different from the Mechanical Age. The things we design will be less constrained by the physical, and more dependent on imagination and expression – on culture. The workings of mechanical machines are obvious: pull a lever here, press another there, fill up the boiler, adjust the pressure. Actions have an overt relationship to what happens. Electro-mechanical machines operate more opaquely, but still the actions needed to control them bear a logical relation to the physical changes necessary for their operation: a contact here, varying resistors there.

Seeing the inner workings of a computer, by contrast, would give us few clues to its operation: there are no necessary correspondences between the controls and their feedback – we can program it to appear as whatever we like. Throwing away a file on our computer might result in a few words on the screen confirming what we have done, or a cartoon of a little dustbin getting fatter as we throw things into it. Neither bears any relationship to the electronic pulses going on in the machine; they are just different ways of representing the system so we can understand what it is and how to use it. As far as a user is concerned, the representation – the user-interface – *is* the system. Some representations of information allow us to grasp its import more or less effortlessly, others actually impede our understanding.

The user-interface gives users of a system a conceptual model of what it is and how it will behave. Naturally this should derive from the system itself but it also needs to take account of what people are likely to bring to it – their experience, preconceptions, abilities and so on, and their needs – what they want to do with it. Early human-computer interfaces were conceived as control panels to a machine. But the graphically-sophisticated screen representations now possible allow a different relationship between the system and its representation, one that is richer and more expressive. Interface designers need to spin a 'narrative', the story they want the user to believe about what the product is and how it will behave.

Interface narrative for the office worker

A good example of the power of narrative is the Macintosh Desktop interface. The Desktop interface was originally designed by Xerox, an experimental system designed not for technologists but for professional people working in offices, people who were not interested in computers, but in getting on with their work. It was designed so that they could learn how to use it in an hour or so. The 'narrative' here is that the system works in a similar way to a person's desk. So documents go into folders; documents you no longer want are thrown in the waste bin, and so on. This narrative is coherent, particularly for its intended audience, office workers.

The concept works well. In the Macintosh version, moreover, it has been delightfully crafted. Some people love their Macs. This is partly due to the graphics which are elegant, simple and restrained (as is appropriate for something that is the background to people's work) and also to do with its 'tone of voice' both graphically, and verbally, in the dialogues with the user. Designers here considered *qualities* of interaction as well as practicalities.

Other good examples in the electronic fields are much more difficult to find. Most companies are not using interaction designers at all. Bad examples abound. The video recorder: why are so many VCR owners unable to program their machine? Bad design. Telecommanders: as you sit in the semi-darkness watching TV, why can't you find the right button? Bad design. Why do many visitors to London's Underground fail to use the ticket machine to buy a ticket? Bad design. Why do the dials on my double oven map inversely to the arrangement of the ovens so every now and then when we go to eat our dinner we find it as raw as it went in? You could say crass stupidity! I say the user is never stupid – another case of bad design.

These examples could have been improved with ordinary designerly commonsense, about people and about the presentation of information. Basic information design techniques such as grouping similar elements, showing order through position and so on, have been ignored. Their design has been from the point of view of the efficiency of the system and its manufacture without much thought for the user's convenience, let alone pleasure

Bad design lacks an organising idea

A more serious problem, though, is that these examples lack an organising idea, a narrative, to let the user grasp what is going on. Or, in the case of the ticket machine, the narrative does not square with the way the machine actually works. For instance, when you arrive at the station and need a ticket your destination is foremost in your mind. The message of the machine, inferred from a distance, is that it sells tickets to stations, each represented by a button. So far so good. Unfortunately, when you find the button for your

Telephone answering machine by Durrell Bishop has a novel 'narrative' interface: the messages are marbles

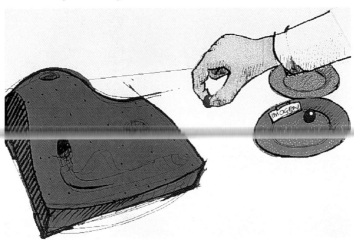

station and press it, the machine takes no notice. It is asking you what ticket type you want (only you haven't noticed the message). Thus starts the loop of misunderstanding – and some poor people never get a ticket out.

The products I have described could all have been improved with the common sense of existing design disciplines such as graphic and product design, film and animation. But these existing languages – graphic, formal, audio-visual – do not fully exploit the possibilities offered by interactive products and systems. Interactivity, that particular quality enabled by the microprocessor, needs a new language, new conventions, which derive from the qualities of the medium. There is a parallel here with film language. In early films, conventions from other media were employed: the camera pointed at the 'stage', the action divided into 'chapters'. Later, people like DW Griffths and Sergei Eisenstein developed a new language of film which sprang from the qualities of the moving image. Today we are at the silent film stage in interaction design, depending on existing design languages to represent systems to users. Multimedia 'books', for instance, are only a transitional phase before new languages and conventions emerge – by accident or design. The Computer Related Design department at the Royal College of Art in London is encouraging designers from many different disciplines to explore what the language of interactivity might be.

Moving from engineering to interaction

Until recently, the driving force behind interactive products and systems has been the engineering – which is truly remarkable. It has been difficult enough to get systems to work at all, let alone think about *the way* they work. But this is changing, for technological reasons as well as marketing ones. The first systems were designed by engineers for people like themselves, other engineers and scientists.

The next stage was computers for office workers – knowledge workers – who were interested in computers as tools for their work, not in the computers themselves. The graphical user interface, like the Macintosh or Microsoft Windows, enabled people to have a user interface that could be in the language of their work, rather than that of the computer. Rather than having to adjust to the computer and remember arbitrary commands, the computer was adjusted to them. As graphic displays allowed the interface to become expressive, new levels of communication with users became possible – and necessary. Suggestion, emotion, aesthetic qualities were inferred by people whether designers intended them or not. So now the qualities of interaction need to be *designed,* not left to chance. Which is where designers come in.

Designers cannot sit on the sidelines. They need to become involved in the design of interactive products – information and entertainment systems, electronic products, responsive environments. Our world is being transformed by these technologies and designers need to be there, making things beautiful as well as practical, expressive as well as functional. Whether we like it or not, culture in the next century will be conditioned by electronics and telecommunications. Artists and designers need to be players, not spectators.

A well-developed desire for individuality

Sir Terence Conran ENGLAND

Former Chairman of Storehouse plc and founder of Habitat and the Conran Design Group, **Sir Terence Conran** is also founder and Chairman of London's Design Museum. He now has a 25 per cent stake in Fitch plc, one of the UK's leading design consultancies, and runs several acclaimed London restaurants. Conran's achievements have been recognised by bodies including the Royal College of Art, the Chartered Society of Designers and D&AD. In 1992 he was made a Commandeur des Arts et des Lettres by Jack Lang, then Minister of Culture and Education in France.

Mass production in robot factories will meet basic human needs. But the real future for designers lies elsewhere – in using imagination and skill to respond to a growing desire for individuality in niche markets.

There is no doubt that the design of products can play a vital part in helping to drag the world out of recession, just as Raymond Loewy and Walter Dorwin Teague helped to revive the American economy in the 1930s. Their 'optimistic' streamlined products stimulated consumer desire for change and helped to get the great American productive machine back into gear once again.

That is exactly what the world economy needs again today. But we face a very different scenario. On one side we have a disgust for the excesses of consumerism that we witnessed during the 1980s. We believe that less is more, we want products that are of better quality and consequently last longer. We are environmentally and ecologically concerned about the despoiling of the earth and the diminution of its resources. And yet we realise that if man is to have a reason for his existence on this planet then he must have an opportunity to make some sort of contribution. To do this, he has to work and has to make things.

Design at the crossroads

Undoubtedly we are at some sort of crossroads as a rapid increase in inventions and new technologies have a vast impact on the designer, influencing not only what he designs but the way he designs it. But there is also a vast change in manufacturing methods: automation and robotics can make much more with far fewer people employed.

So what is the solution? I believe that it can lie in the hands of designers and marketeers. Basic consumer needs will obviously be satisfied by vast automated factories that mass-produce products to satisfy the *needs* of the majority of people at the lowest possible price. Design certainly plays an essential role in this scenario in perfecting the style and efficiency which allows products to satisfy the mass market.

Stimulating and satisfying people's *wants* for products that perhaps they didn't know they desired is far more complex and it may provide the solution to the problem of employment in the future. I believe that it is perfectly possible that once people's needs are adequately taken care of, then it is natural for them to *want* products that have characteristics that satisfy their desire to make an individualistic statement about themselves and reflect their own personality and position in society.

Only in this way can we break down manufacturing into relatively efficient units once again, and only in this way can we keep creativity alive and employ those people who want to work and want to leave a mark on the world they inhabit.

The role of designers in this scenario is vital because it is with their knowledge, skill and imagination that market niches can be explored and consumer desire for change exploited. In this way small industries can be created, hands and brains can be kept busy, and economies can be ebullient.

There is plenty of evidence to show that in an educated society there is already a well-developed desire for individuality. It is in the interest of designers, manufacturers, distributors, educationalists and governments to see that this desire for change and the stimulation of unexpressed wants is satisfied. Only in this way will responsible consumerism survive, trade and employment be created, and designers have projects to work on.

Corbusian Everytown in the British film Things to Come (1936),
written by HG Wells and designed by Vincent Korda

Section 5:
Visions of the future

Designers, by the nature of their work, live on the very edge of change, but recognising the larger meaning of future trends is never easy to do. The final section of this book is devoted to visions of the future, to putting those final all-important pieces of the jigsaw together to understand the whole picture. It is a theme which suffused a great many of the debates at Design Renaissance. Cinematic visions of the future over the past century have always mistrusted technology and argued that science ends in tears, as **Christopher's Frayling's** entertaining journey through movieland demonstrates. But back in the real world, things are fast becoming unreal. **Derrick de Kerckhove** argues that the virtuality of the electronic age is changing objective reality so fast, trashing both time and place, that the responsibility of design in the future will be to make the *real* world worth living in. This theme is explored in greater depth by **Michael Brill** in his analysis of the changes in office work where the 'virtual office' already confuses three-dimensional design traditionalists. Some fashionable design visions of the future are expertly deconstructed. Robot factory workers won't take over the world, says **Peter Mowforth**. Neither will the electric car, predicts **Richard Seymour**. The final word, however, goes to **Yuri Soloviev**, once a leading technocrat in the Soviet Union, who reminds us that reading the future depends on understanding the past. **Soloviev** believes that science can be tamed and that designers have a key role to play in complex projects in the next century because they alone can integrate art and technology. It is a positive note on which to end.

Design, interactivity and the production of meaning

Derrick de Kerckhove CANADA

Derrick de Kerckhove is Director of the McLuhan Program in Culture and Technology at the University of Toronto in Canada and is a consultant in media, cultural interests and related policies. His most recent book, *Brainframes: Technology, Mind, and Business* (1991), addresses the differences between the effect of TV, computers and hypermedia on corporate culture, business practices and economic markets.

In an age of interactive systems and new electronic media, when meaning is no longer homogenous and time and space have been trashed, design matters more than ever to tame technology and make the newly emerging global psychology worth living for.

At the dawn of Western civilisation, Aeschylus's *Prometheus Bound* revealed the West's deepest secret. Nobody heard it, but it is still there in the archives of the world. The invention of letters made technology the basis of the Western cultures: *Syntheseis ton grammaton, mousometor,* the assembly of letters, mother of the muses, mother of invention. The alphabetic code was like the genetic code, a system available for recombination and engineering. It was the source of all blueprints and all inventions in the West; it was also the most powerful model for digitisation. The alphabet would one day lead to digitisation as the natural consequence of dividing reality in meaningless but extremely modular bits.

Today, thanks precisely to digitisation, design takes over. The binary code can translate anything into anything else, forms, textures, sounds, feelings, even smell, and why not taste soon? Design is the essence of simulation and representation, hence its ominous responsibility to simulate properly and represent usefully.

Governments are beginning to grant design a renewed attention because many people sense that design bridges technology and psychology and that the economy will depend on design as an interpreter of technology and as an inspiration for technological development in a software environment.

However, when governments take interest in design, it is time to watch out. When it is abused rather than just used, design can and has served some rather questionable political functions, such as propaganda (70 years of Communism amounting to naught, five years of raging war in Europe, over 40 million dead both at the front and in the background).

Advertising, a minor form of propaganda and a major component of design, is partly responsible for the tacit war waged on the environment by accelerated consumption and the creation and support of artificial needs. Even social engineering can be the downside of design, as in the urban wastelands its Modernist ambitions generated in a very short term.

Now we hear from Stefano Marzano, Ezio Manzini and others at the Design

Renaissance congress that the design industry should become political. It always has been, so it is refreshing that now it will become self-consciously so. However, if that is the case, then we ought to be as informed as possible about the relationship between design, technology and the social construction and production of meaning.

A world before interaction

In the old days, before design became necessary, technology was tame and obedient, and life was evenly paced. There was a real world out there called 'objective', and there was a real person right here, called 'subjective', and there were a lot of printed words to bring order to their relationships. Things were simple, at least in the industrial countries founded on alphabetic literacy, because there was a human and environment polarity, and one pole was constantly evolving and adapting while the other remained stable. Or at least appeared so. This was the blessed time of non-interactivity; time and space were fixed, and minds and bodies were free to roam without losing their bearing.

But then, with the unstoppable ingenious innovations of engineering, the pace began to quicken. The telegraph helped create remote-control markets (with their attending accelerated need for production and distribution of goods) and colonies. The radio generated mass audiences, economies of scale and early stirrings of the advertising industry supported by the press. And then television provided a post-war delivery system for accelerated war-time production, which meant a massive increase in the numbers of the buying public.

Among other demographic developments, women had entered the workforce and begun to appear in political, economic and public life (even as their images were being sold on TV). However, nothing, apart from the evident speeding of society, seemed to have changed; that is because none of the above media was interactive.

Surely it is a fast world, but still the same polarity prevailed; from mobile human to stable – if accelerated – environment. The Gulf War was perhaps the last time television was given full range, albeit under the tightest control ever practised by design, for the one-way production of meaning. In the words of Augustin Berque: 'If the world said OK to the crusade against Saddam (Hussein), it is not only because the world drinks Coca Cola. It is because, to a large extent, the meaning of today's world finds its source, its creation and its distribution in the USA'. But the era of television, of a mass creation of meaning, is over. The time has come for the interactive creation of meaning and that is the fundamental paradigmatic shift in social discourse.

Fundamental shift in relationships

By 1991, personal computers had already stolen the attention of a full generation from the seduction of the TV screen. By 1991, computers were already celebrating what has become known as 'convergence', the greatest technological marriage of all times, with the telephone (the most powerful of the unsung technologies of communication). The fundamental polarity had changed. Humans were mobile, active, changing – but so was the increasingly intelligent environment that machines were creating.

The old comfortable relationship between subjects and objects was challenged. Strange new breeds of consciousness had begun to flourish with interactive systems: real-time self-adjusting databases; rapid updating of political statements via polling and spin-doctoring; intermediate, anonymous, asynchronous, mind collectives on nets, usenets, newsnets, eathernets and internets; distributed parallel processing; self-adjusting learning expert systems with neural networks.

And to make matters even more complicated, both time and space are now being trashed in 'real-time' technologies and 'virtual reality' machines. With virtual reality, interactivity brings renewed considerations about time in space. We are losing ground. Not content to argue with our screens, after decades of passive acceptance of their dictatorship, we now feel the need to penetrate them, to plunge into them as so many Ulysses beckoned by the siren calls in an ocean of electrons.

From now on, between the subject and the object is the traject, the pattern of transmission or travel. Now that we share our privacy with world-distributed databanks, we have to add another mental being to the construction of our own private mind, the interjective. We are both statistics and persons all at once. Our prized psychological legacy, our personal 'point-of-view' – the greatest gift of the greatest designers, the painters and architects of the Renaissance and after – is now being challenged by a much deeper, much larger, much more intimate and intense, and perhaps intimidating, perception, that of our 'point-of-being'.

The deepest thought of Marshall McLuhan, in my opinion, was not 'The medium is the message'. It is the lesser known, equally succinct, more enigmatic statement: 'In the electronic age, we wear all mankind as our skin.' Indeed the world is not 'out there' anymore, it is right here, under my skin.

The other fundamental paradigmatic shift accompanying interactivity is the shift from visual to tactile sensory processing. While the printing press generated strings of data affecting our visual processing strategies and bringing on perspective as the distantiated, objective spatial arrangement for our personal information processing, electronic media are bringing the world and what we still call reality right into our bodies as extensions of our central nervous system. Interactivity is a technical term for the extensions of our proprioceptive and tactile relationships to the environment.

Creating an intelligible environment

The result of all this is that we are all – including designers – frightfully confused. The creation of meaning is not homogenous anymore; ideologies have been thoroughly trashed along with the Berlin Wall; TV is henceforth too decentralised to pretend to the status of a 'public mind' anymore; and in some way, which does indeed recall the heyday of the first Renaissance, when people began to make up their own minds with the rapid spread of books, we cannot let other people or institutions do our thinking for us; we are under the responsibility of creating meaning ourselves in our much mediated dialogue with the world.

Is all this leading to a political platform for the design industry? Perhaps not directly, but it is to artists and designers that more and more people will turn to ask for an intelligible and livable technological environment; it is designers and artists who they will ask to be comprehensive in their approach to reality; it is from designers and artists that we could expect a new vision of civilisation, one addressing the global as well as the local needs. After all, if cities managed to reduce social anarchy to civic order, it was not just the military or the police action, it was largely because architects, planners, restaurateurs, painters, poets, novelists, dramatists and musicians provided from within and did not impose from without, the need and the urge for a social reality that was truly satisfying, if only for short periods of time.

The responsibility of design is to make this world livable, not just for those who have the means, but for all. This is not wishful thinking, not rhetorical; it is the expression of a very strong feeling that, if they are supported by enlightened design with the greater good and the larger reach of people and the greatest respect of differing cultures in mind, the contents of our newly developing global psychology will be thrilling and worth living for.

Wild times in the world of office work

Michael Brill USA

Michael Brill is President of BOSTI (the Buffalo Organisation for Social and Technological Innovation) and Professor of Architecture at the State University of New York at Buffalo. He spent 10 years designing hospitals, housing, offices, theatres and interiors before shifting his focus to research and consultancy. BOSTI measures the effects of design management and advises organisations on the development of high performance workplaces. Brill is the author of *Using Office Design to Increase Productivity*.

Global business forces and new technology are transforming the office of the white-collar worker. The result: massive changes in organisational structure and culture. But as corporations are fundamentally reinvented, how should office design and planning respond to the new landscape of work?

Certain changes in the world of white-collar work are happening to all workers everywhere, driven by global business forces. Following a 40-year period of modern-office evolution, we are now experiencing very rapid, almost revolutionary change in the four basic components of office work: the work's structure, the workforce, the worktools, and the workplace.

Organisational structure is becoming more team-based, more customer-focused, more entrepreneurial and nimble. The workforce is getting smaller, changing its profile, and undergoing rapid professionalisation. Technology is becoming more portable, more friendly, more ubiquitous, more integrated, and more powerful (and paradoxically, we are just learning how to use it). And finally, the workplace is being reconceptualised more as a tool, and used as such – and certain types of workplaces and spaces are becoming more important.

This essay examines the effects of the first three trends on design of the workplace. These trends are certainly being propelled by our current difficult economic climate, but even when the economy changes they will persist because they are a fundamental restructuring (and not mere tinkering), and because they have demonstrable benefits.

To stay competitive, many organisations are now engaged in a fundamental and radical redesign of their business processes, sometimes called re-engineering. The outcome is often an organisation with a new shape, frequently of fully autonomous self-managing teams. Most outcomes embody one basic idea, that the people who do the work should have the authority, resources and capability to change to suit the customer. In a re-engineered company, ongoing changes are normal and welcomed.

Organisational structure
The 'deconstruction' of larger organisations involves the creation of smaller, more nimble pieces, with these new pieces being quite autonomous, more focused

on a carefully defined portion of the business and more responsive to market shifts and opportunities. With this erosion of the centre, certain workspaces and workforces (other than those at headquarters) become more important.

The important new places are where products are created (such as the workspaces of product design teams and software engineers); where products are creatively fitted to customers' needs (marketing and sales offices); where people learn new skills and new ways to work (such as training and instructional sites); and virtual office sites (the home office, the airplane, the car-phoned car, the satellite or drop-in office).

The new businesses pay more attention to the ways groups work, emphasising team selection and training, electronic team augmentation and team-based reward systems, as well as new design concepts that truly emphasise and support teamwork. Meanwhile, the virtual corporation, making virtual products, needs a virtual workspace and a virtual workforce. The desire to be rapidly responsive to marketplace nuances creates 'virtuality' in all aspects of work life. The characteristics of virtuality (a term derived from electronics) is that it adapts, always, to whatever you need.

Virtual products and services are ones with high information content and meaningful flexibility, often developed with substantial customer participation – a kind of mass-customisation of products that also have the capacity for further in-use customisation by users. To make these probably requires a virtual corporation, one that focuses its information richness on understanding and anticipating customer needs and adapts to them. Such organisations keep information current and useful by structuring themselves to take advantage of 'partnering' with their suppliers, distributors, retailers and end-users.

These groups are increasingly interactive, inter-penetrating each other's spaces and work, expanding the team concept to its ultimate. A virtual workforce is one that is information rich, always learning, and highly adaptive and mobile. Virtual offices are a set of places that share these qualities as well. We are seeing all these emerge rapidly. No resources stand idle: all should be fully used and available 'just-in-time' and only when they are needed.

A changing workforce

The white collar office-based workforce is getting relatively smaller, compared to the total workforce. It also has a different profile with more women, more professionals, more older people and more highly-educated workers – but with relatively fewer clerical staff, and fewer managers. Everyone acts as a professional. Jobs are becoming more complete and complex: most people have jobs that are far less fragmented, and are asked to be more creative than in the past. They have more authority to make decisions, supported by a richness of electronically-provided information that allows unpredictability and spontaneity to enter work.

Staff training is becoming a major corporate endeavour: constant change coupled with increased responsibility requires fairly continuous training to sustain or increase the quality of individual and team contributions. About

$220 billion was spent on corporate training in the USA in 1992 alone (an amount greater than that spent annually on all college education in the USA). This is predicted to increase five-fold by year 2000. In this context, design of training environments, especially for team training, becomes very important.

People are increasingly being seen as the organisation's primary resource, as 'human capital', and their idiosyncrasies and different ways of working are being honoured and supported.

Performance in a group becomes a major criterion of staff evaluations. Because people work more frequently in teams, their performance in a group becomes more important – and more important to measure. Flexible staffing and flexible scheduling take on special importance, as both seek to provide a 'just-in-time' workforce.

Technological change

The much-vaunted promise of electronic technology that has always been just around the corner may actually be in view. Well-documented studies show that our trillions of dollars of investment in electronic technology has resulted in a 'productivity paradox'. The paradox is that while business technologies have clearly increased the productivity of individuals, these increases do not reappear at any higher level of aggregation, such as the team, division, company, industry or even nation. Somehow, these individual increases get 'lost' – in the linkages and communications among people. So the new emphasis in the organisation of work, and in workplaces and technology, is on: first, connectivity among people – the development and use of 'groupware' that enhances group performance; and second, access to enormous communicative and computational power through vast 'electronic highways'.

Communications are vital to a dispersed workforce. Technology has become more portable, powerful and easier to use. It enables easy mobility and geographic dispersion while doing work. The laptop with fax and modem, the cellular telephone, and networks permit the office to be virtually anywhere, and always open for business.

Capabilities will be added over the next few years as the multi-media, multi-purpose 'electronic briefcase' emerges. But even with all this technology, there will still only be a slow march to the paperless office. There may be much less paper in five to ten years, but not before.

Implications on office planning and design

So what are the implications of all these trends in organisational structure, workforces and technology for the planning and design of the workplace. Some implications are: smaller buildings, in more dispersed locations, and with more variety in character; a new fluidity in working arrangements; more understanding and use of the workspace as a tool; and new offices.

Companies are seeking workspace nearer their customers, in more dispersed locations. Fewer are downtown because of the growth of the new 'super-suburbs', the availability of smaller, suburban satellite offices; the relocation of electronic 'back office' operations to cheaper space outside the central business district, and the growth of various forms of telecommuting.

Existing but under-utilised buildings of odd character will become more usable and more viable in the office market – ones with smaller-than-usual floorplates, with peculiar geometries, or ones built for other purposes, such as warehouses, archives and factories.

There will be less demand for office space because of a shrinking workforce, smaller organisations, and because of substantial space-saving from a new form of office sharing, called 'hotelling'. The current enormous glut of office space will continue. New uses must be found for some of this excess office space. In some cities, older office space is now being re-used as low income housing. In others, office buildings are being converted into residential hotels even before they open their doors as offices.

Technology makes the office wherever you are – the virtual office. Since portable technology can be used both on-the-road and be docked into networks anywhere, electronic work is unhinged from any particular location. Downtown is no longer the privileged location for work. In fact, no place is really privileged. The laptop and cellular telephone permit any place to be a drop-in work centre.

Space newly built for business units will be quite different from 'normal' office space, for it must accommodate the much wider variety of space types needed by vertically integrated and team-based organisations: they need offices, of course, but intermixed with spaces for training, laboratories, workshops, showrooms, media studios, research and development, production – all in one building.

The new furniture systems will be freer, much easier to manipulate by users, and much less rigid about modularity. They will use space efficiently in odd-shaped floorplates, and in non-office settings; they will support new ways of working, and permit user experiments to optimise ways of working.

Periodic residents

Increasingly, many people are out of the office, often 50 to 80 per cent of the time. They are really only 'periodic residents'. Companies want workspace just in time and in the best place, the same lean way they want to use all their resources. Satisfying this organisational desire brings us to some previously unthinkable ways of working. Even the most conservative of companies are seeking highly innovative space-use strategies to reduce the expense of under-utilised space. At the same time, they are seeking ways to design and use workspace to enhance productivity and support teamwork. One model is the office operated like a hotel.

Office sharing among periodic residents only works if just one person is in. When more are in, performance is reduced for all but one of them. Many companies, realising this, now have offices where 'periodic residents' do not 'own' an office, but get an excellent one whenever they are in – like a hotel. They can operate at ratios of, say, five to six periodic residents to one space, offering substantial space savings *and* high-performance workspace.

Hotelling, as it has become known, has many forms. Periodic residents have no permanent workspaces, no fixed work address, but a fixed telephone number that follows them. But individuals still need a 'home-base' fixed-address place to store their stuff while they are out. There is reservation hotelling: periodic residents reserve a first-rate office, for their sole use, before they come in, and return it upon leaving after a day or two. This office is managed by a 'concierge' and service staff who will bring in your stored stuff, set it up, put up your nameplate and your dog's picture. Nomads of Free-Address is a different system: the individual's work materials are stored in mobile furniture, often at the front door, and you move it to and 'dock' it in any empty workspace available. This is a do-it-yourself system; no reservations are required.

Group Address means that while there is a fixed address for the group, individual locations float within the larger space. The area may contain offices, but there is a strong focus on teamwork spaces. Red Carpet Clubs, meanwhile, emulate those in the airports. Instead of having all the office functions you need in one space (the office), it is possible to separate functions into separate areas, each better designed for that one task. In such a scheme, people use a mix of task-specific work settings on a drop-in basis that may include work-lounges, meeting spaces, super-telephone booths, common areas and shared services.

Many people will have 'real' work-at-home offices, some heavily used by telecommuters. Expect new homes to be built with a workspace, zoned from living space, with private entrance, and access to networks. The virtual office, meanwhile, is really the 'no-office office', where people work anywhere and anytime out of their electronic briefcase, and there may be no preferred location for work or several preferred locations.

Workplace as a tool

Organisations are paying increased attention to their workplaces because research results show that better planning and design has economic leverage: workplace design really affects individual, group and organisational performance. Also, real savings can be made through various forms of hotelling, and, by implication, other facilities innovation. In the new organisations, groups and individuals must have more control over the tools they use. Since the workplace is a tool, it should be designed and furnished to be used in the quest to find the best ways to work. Places where people meet are increasingly valued places. While office work is certainly being powerfully transformed by technology, the 'productivity paradox' suggests that interaction among people is becoming more critical. So places where people form groups, work in teams and even where they have random face-to-face encounters becomes highly valued.

With many individuals out of the office with their laptops, the workplace will be designed more and more for social purposes: for transmission of process or how-to information (which requires face-to-face contact); for creative teaming; for social renewal; and for negotiation and persuasion, where reading faces and body language means a lot. So we can expect more corporate questioning of the business value of high-style and image-based design. If not much of a business case can be found, businesses will insist on places that are more function-based and business-based than image-based.

Today's most prominent style, the 'corporate look', with its linear, regular, uniform, hierarchical neatness that hides work, is quite incompatible with the new dynamics, pragmatics and realities of work. In business units and self-managing teams, we now find much more product 'presence' in the workspace, so it looks more like a home-workshop than an office. With the new, more supple furniture, teams and individuals are developing a 'high-involvement' look – an environment that really supports how they work.

More focused flexibility

In the face of what seems to be rapid and continuous change, we are moving (strangely but appropriately) away from total flexibility as a design strategy. While there is much organisational change, a decade of it shows there is a common direction and a predictable trajectory. This allows us to sort out what needs to be flexible, and what does not. Organisational structures are very fluid, and organisations right now cannot much predict their shapes even a few months into the future. To design for universal flexibility is too expensive, and quite unnecessary, and constant physical change is a nightmare for the company.

Given this uncertainty, companies are moving towards well-considered but fairly fixed generic floor plans. These have: a more 'constructed' interior architecture with many specific spaces built as fixed, but with high flexibility in some portions of fixed space; relocation flexibility coming from moving people, not offices, and from electronic switching, rather than pulling wires; fixed spines which distribute power, communications, and climate control; and individual workspaces which fit all needs with just one or two sizes.

In the new, flatter, more entrepreneurial organisations, and in ones where teamwork has become as important as that of individual contributors, there is a movement away from status-based design to function-based design. Our past and continued emphasis on workspaces for individuals has tended to limit our design exploration of places used by groups and those used by everybody (like lounges, corridors, lobbies and parking lots). The computer industry is developing 'groupware' – hardware and software that tries to beat the 'productivity paradox' by providing powerful electronic augmentation of group processes. Design of the workplace itself can be a form of groupware through thoughtful design of group-use spaces such as high-performance project rooms or team suites.

Many places are workspaces. If you observe where people really have their work-related discussion, you will discover work going on in the hallway, the parking lot, just outside the front door, near the fax machine, in the coffee room, and just outside the big conference room right after the conference. All of this activity can be supported through design. As organisations reinvent themselves, this is the task of the office designer and planner.

Yesterday's tomorrows

Christopher Frayling ENGLAND

Christopher Frayling is Head of the School of Humanities and Pro-Rector of the Royal College of Art in London. He is an historian, critic and broadcaster and has published numerous books and articles on the popular arts. He is Chairman of the Visual Arts Panel of the Arts Council of Great Britain and a Trustee of the Victoria and Albert Museum, London.

Cinematic visions of the future – from Metropolis *to* Robocop *– provide a rich insight into human fears about the dark transformation of the city by science and machines. The movies may be a high-tech medium but the message for the past 100 years has been that technology is bound to end in tears.*

'The future', wrote Arthur C Clarke, the author of *2001: a Space Odyssey,* 'is not what it used to be'! And there is no doubt that yesterday's visions of what the future might look and feel like are strangely appealing – compared with what the future actually looks and feels like. Yesterday's tomorrows, from late nineteenth century illustrations of the latest discoveries (so beloved by the Surrealists), via Eastern European robots, the Dymaxion House and the New York World's Fair of the inter-war years, to comics and Saturday morning serials in the 1950s, have long proved a rich resource for artists and designers.

But *cinematic* depictions of yesterday's tomorrows, because we can re-live and re-evaluate them every time we view the films or videos, are more than just a visual resource. They can also tell us about a whole range of popular conceptions and misconceptions. Whether the films function as myths (sorting out contradictions which are on the audience's mind) or as products (trying hard not to offend the paying customers), they have often contained a strange alliance of conservative thinking with radical visuals and techniques – not unlike automobiles, a parallel industry. Consequently they provide a unique insight into 'common knowledge' concerning maps of the future.

Mad bad and dangerous to know

Various themes have recurred, over and over again, ever since the origins of cinema. *Fictional* scientists, technologists and designers tend to be presented as mad, bad and dangerous to know – they belong to a select band of researchers led by Doctors Faustus, Frankenstein, Jekyll and Strangelove. *Factual* scientists, technologists and designers tend to be presented as loveable (if difficult to live with), saintly and public-spirited – like Mickey Rooney as young Thomas Edison, Spencer Tracey as the grown-up one, and Edward G Robinson as the man who found a cure for syphilis in *Dr Ehrlich's Magic Bullet,* or RJ Mitchell, the man who designed the Spitfire, played by Leslie Howard as a charming donnish type in a blazer.

Most visions of the future tend to be dystopian (it is going to get worse)

163

rather than utopian (it is going to get better): the great high-technology medium of the cinema has spent much of its hundred-year history telling the audience that technological development is bound to end in tears. Today, in films which are full of computer-generated imagery, computer buffs tend to be presented as bespectacled, nerdy sociopaths.

However, some visions of the future (especially in the 1920s and 1930s, but also, in more popular films in America in the 1950s) have shown a strong faith in modernity and (in rarer cases) Modernism. *Things to Come* (1936), an unusual example of an optimistic – well, almost – version of the future, based as it is on HG Wells' blend of socialism and electricity, stands out from the tradition. In Hollywood films of the 1930s, *moderne* styles often tended to be associated with a) high living and luxury and b) gangsters: old money preferred wood-panelling and paintings of horses. In 1950s sci-fi films, modern machines were fun in a whoopee sort of way, but as the white-coated physicist opined in the last reel, things are certain to go wrong 'if we continue to tamper with the forces of nature'.

The most interesting of yesterday's tomorrows have included some reflections on what science and technology (*and* scientists and technologists) might be like; in other words they have included a model of social and technological change. Others – the majority – have been content with white zipper-suits, wooden dialogue, and gung-ho machines. Oddly enough, the latter, refracted through Camp, may have made the stronger visual impact.

Visions of the modern city

The modern city has been presented – on the dystopia/utopia axis – as *either* a sinful alternative to the idyllic life of the countryside and the open range (most Westerns are based on this contrast) *or* a place of unprecedented excitement and possibility where all that is solid melts into the air (Soviet films of the 1920s were fond of this vision of modernity).

In the last 20 years, visions of the city in big budget films have all been of the 'future shock' variety: a positive image is today inconceivable. Everything about the city – from its streets, to its buildings, to its transportation systems, to its public conveniences – has become a place of danger. And it is *All The Fault Of The Corporation,* a message which is paradoxically brought to you by *The Corporation* itself.

Bearing these themes in mind, let us take a journey through Yesterday's Tomorrows – according to the cinema. In Georges Méliès' *Channel Tunnel* ('an Anglo-French nightmare', made in 1906), the scientists are umbrella-waving lunatics, the French are a long way ahead of the Brits, and the images are reminiscent of *fin de siècle* illustrated magazines. In Fritz Lang's *Metropolis* (1926), the city is sectored, in descending order, into rococo roof dwellings (where the rich live), skyscrapers, machine rooms (the future is a nightmare based on the steam and pistons of manufacturing industry, rather than on electronics and digits) and the workers' city where all the dwellings are identical: houses for the rich, housing for the poor. The moral of the film is trite by today's standards:

Fritz Lang's Metropolis (1926): the nightmare of the machine

if only the head (the bosses), the heart (the hero) and the hand (the workers) would get together, everything would be all right. But the design, a collaboration of painters, engineers and architects, has weathered well.

Lang's *Woman in the Moon* (1930) introduced the modern 'look' to rockets (one of its technical advisers was the young Werner Von Braun) and invented the idea of the countdown. In FW Murnau's *Sunrise* (1927), the city – with its jazz, its trams, and its jostling crowds – is contrasted very unfavourably with the peasant village: while in Dziga Vertov's *Man with the Movie Camera* (1929), the city, as seen and reconstructed by the 'kino-eye', is a place of movement, multi-dimensionality and potential; the city, after all, was where the Revolution began (as depicted in the careful geography of Serge Eisenstein's *October,* completed the previous year).

The opening reels of Charlie Chaplin's *Modern Times* (1936) have provided some of the most enduring images of automation and the assembly-line, two of the key icons of 'modernity'. Designed by Norwich architect Danny Hall, the giant cog-wheels and conveyor-belts also function as a parody of *Metropolis*. When Charlie finds himself chucked out into the street, he picks up a stick from the ground – unaware that there is a red flag attached to it – and unwittingly leads a workers' march.

In the same year, William Cameron Menzies directed *Things to Come* with its prediction of the London blitz, and its vision of 'Everytown' in the year 2036: this vision was based by designer Vincent Korda on Le Corbusier (who had been approached for architectural ideas, but had turned the producers down), and was put together with a little help from Moholy Nagy, who happened to be in London at the time. Not many of Moholy's concepts made their way into the finished film (a few bubbling retorts, and men in diving suits seen through corrugated glass), but they were recently discovered in their entirety in a rusting can of film.

Things to Come contains a gleaming white vision of the future. It at least *attempts* a debate on 'which shall it be?' (science or humanity?) It also includes a glimpse of the young Victor Papanek – then a schoolboy – dutifully greeting Ralph Richardson with the words 'here comes the Boss'. After 1936, such gleaming visions of the future – with their monorails and all-electric labour-saving kitchens and early shopping malls – tended to surface mainly in World Fairs and Expos, where their purpose became promotional rather than philosophical.

Predictions of the doomsters
By the 1970s and 1980s, Yesterday's Tomorrows had begun to reflect as well as visualise 'green' debates and the predictions of the doomsters: in Richard Fleischer's *Soylent Green* (1973), the great revelation is that the staple diet in New York – at a time in the future of famine and environmental destruction – is dried, recycled people. In Ridley Scott's *Bladerunner* (1984), Los Angeles is drenched in acid rain, audio traffic signals shout at passers-by, cars are retro-fitted with bolt-on parts, and buildings wear their duct-work on the outside – as Raymond Chandler, the presiding genius of the film, put it, 'the streets were dark with something more than night'. And in Paul Verhoeven's *Robocop* (1987), the mechanical/virtual policeman sorts out inner-city problems with extreme prejudice, while the children play 'Nuke 'Em' in their living rooms.

'Which shall it be?', intones Raymond Massey – in his sharp-shouldered Samurai outfit – at the end of *Things to Come*. Gleaming white or acid rain? The all-electric kitchen or recycled people? Mechanical or electronic? Corporations or oak-tree democracies? Design for Profit or Design for Need? Dark Ages or Renaissance? Umbrella-waving lunatics or boffins or ... what? One thing's for sure: Renaissances are exciting and invigorating and all very well, but *keep watching the skies...*

Ridley Scott's Bladerunner (1984): the city as a place of danger

Evolution of the robot

Peter Mowforth SCOTLAND

Peter Mowforth is a founding Director of the Turing Institute in Glasgow and has been responsible for both the robot and vision laboratories. He is currently Director of Research with responsibilities for the research, development and application engineering activities within the company. He has published more than 70 research papers on artificial intelligence, and is Chairman of the International Robot Games Committee.

Robots can be programmed to beat a Grand Master at chess, but they fail at the simplest tasks requiring a mimickry of natural intelligence. Now the future for robotics lies in hard automation, smart robot-navigated cars and the entertainment business – which is where it all started 70 years ago.

Directly or indirectly, technology uses tricks from nature which are interpreted and manufactured to provide products which give humans some new enjoyment, skill or edge. The primary role for design is either to define the efficiency and costs for manufacture or to pre-define how well it will be used. Given that virtually all technology is to be used directly by humans, the quality of design maps directly onto the success of its use by humans. In this way, design must not be confused with art. The purpose of art is not to mimic nature. It is to comment on it and the humanity that exists within it. Hence, issues of aesthetics, appearance or style are of secondary importance.

Nowhere are these issues of design and functionality so confusing as when we attempt to build 'artificial'[1] life forms solely with technology. The result is a subject full of misunderstandings, myths and idiosyncrasies. The subject is called robotics and the purpose of this short essay is to try to provide the lay reader with a brief glimpse into this fascinating and controversial area.

For thousands of years, humans have toyed with the notion of artificial mechanical life forms. The ancient Greeks built statues whose parts could be moved using steam power. In the eighteenth and nineteenth centuries, both Britain and Japan built many sophisticated clockwork automata whose primary purpose was entertainment and amusement. In the 1920s, a Czech stage play *Rossum's Universal Robots* introduced the term 'robot', derived from the Czech word meaning worker, to mean a mechanical man. The steel woman in the film *Metropolis* or the tin man in *The Wizard of Oz* further ingrained the concept of robotics, as did Asimov's *I Robot* and later books. The important point to note is that although the word robot might have its meaning derived from work, the evolving reality was of a technology linked directly with the world of entertainment.

Steel-collared workforce

It was not until the late 1950s that the first industrial robots appeared. The leading pioneer of these early technologies, Joseph Engelberger, failed to win much interest for his work in the US and almost another decade passed before the re-industrialised Japanese took interest, largely as the result of a chronic shortage of skilled workers. However, it was not until the 1980s and the infamous front cover of *Time* magazine which proclaimed that a new steel-collared workforce was on the move and that we could all look forward to significantly increased leisure time, that the hype started in earnest.

In the early eighties, many companies involved with robotics saw their share-price rocket and order-books fill. For those in industry and commerce the word robot meant what its Czech derivation suggested. Unfortunately, by the mid-1980s, the steel-collared worker was showing signs of tarnishing.

Whilst their protagonists claimed them to be the universal, programmable worker, the truth was that they were typically expensive, difficult to change job and prone to breaking down. As to universal, they were almost universally deaf, dumb, blind and stupid. The technology proved successful in a few niche areas such as welding and paint spraying but more often spectacularly failed in areas where manipulating things, perceiving things or having to redo things was what was needed. Obviously, we needed to make our robots smart.

Throughout the 1980s very large sums of money were spent by governments and industries throughout the world in an attempt to make industrial robots smart. The bottom line was one of dramatic failure. In several industries robots have now been replaced by special-purpose machines, or firms have returned to using cheap labour combined with products that are better designed for the manufacturing process. Of course there are notable exceptions. The point is that very much less than one per cent of manufacturing worldwide is performed by robots. So what went wrong? Where did we underestimate the problem?

Failed domestic servants

Imagine that you went to a consortium of the most technically advanced companies in the world and asked for two quotes. The first would be for a robot that would guarantee to make your breakfast every morning and then clear-up afterwards. The second would be to fly to Mars. I suggest that the first quote would be very much more expensive and the delivery time very much longer. The reason is that we know how to solve the second problem and have done it – not so the first.

Just because most humans are perfectly able to do this does not mean that it is easy. Let us briefly examine some of the tasks that might be required of our imaginary servant. The robot would have to hear and understand what you wanted for breakfast. There is no technology in the world that can perfectly recognise human speech in a normal, conversational style.

Second, if the robot heard a request for scrambled eggs, consider some of the tasks it would have to accomplish. Finding the eggs, cracking the eggs, removing any broken shell, whisking, melting butter and then evenly cooking the mixture and serving. There is no robot in the world capable of any one of these tasks in a normal domestic kitchen. The chance of combining all these tasks with those of providing coffee, orange juice and toast makes any chance

*Robug from Portsmouth Polytechnic – a wall-climbing competitor in
the International Robot Olympics – is coached by human trainer*

169

of success dwindle. The robot cannot assume that 'things are where they are supposed to be' – human environments are just not like that.

A future for robots

Is there any future for robotics? I suggest that the steel-collared workers of the 1980s will evolve in three different directions. I also suspect that in each area they are likely to succeed well. The idea behind the industrial robot was that of a general purpose machine. Forget about the general purpose bit and simply concentrate on building dedicated, special purpose machines. This is termed hard automation. These machines are now leading the way in high-quality, high-volume, low-cost manufacture by most of the leading manufacturing companies in the world.

The second area for exploitation will be in embedded robotic technology. This will involve transplanting some of the technologies that we might have hoped to find in our general purpose robot, fine-tuning them and then putting them into a niche application. If our imaginary breakfast-making robot were not to fall foul of stray furniture, briefcases or dogs, it would have had to use a vision system to find a clear path on which to navigate. Such technology is now being developed for a future generation of 'smart' cars that will eventually be able to help navigate a vehicle and lower the risk of accidents.

The final area is back to where we started: entertainment. Modern theme parks and museums are starting to make extensive use of animated mechanisms with the appearance and behaviour of animals or imaginary creatures. Such devices are being used extensively on TV and in films with simplified versions starting to become available in toy shops. The recent formation of the International Robot Games Committee to co-ordinate the development of robot competitions provides education and focus for robot builders and entertainment for the public. Such Olympian ideals take us back full circle to where we started with the moving statues of ancient Greece.

The evolution of robots should not come as any surprise. The fact that copying nature often turns out to be much harder than was first expected should be taken as a humbling experience. Smart computers have helped produce chess machines that can beat Grand Masters, diagnose specific diseases better than the most skilled doctors and outperform dealers in the key financial markets. In all these situations, tackling the 'intellectual' problem proved relatively easy. The really tricky bit is in connecting the intellectual solution to our real worlds.

References
1. It is as hard to define an 'artificial' life form as it is to define a 'natural' one. The distinction cannot simply be one of 'manmade' – because so are babies. Selective breeding of farm animals and genetic engineering in test tubes further erodes any chance of a clear distinction.

Motown versus The Dreamers

Richard Seymour ENGLAND

Richard Seymour formed the consultancy Seymour Powell with his partner Dick Powell in 1984. The company has a staff of 22 and concentrates on the areas of new product development and the design of consumer products. Seymour originally trained as a graphic designer and has practised widely within the advertising industry. He has received numerous awards including two D&AD Silvers. His major projects include the Norton FI Motorcycle.

Optimistic visions of the future place the electric car at the centre of a new age of ecologically-benign transport systems. But vested interests, technological limitations, ingrained habits and lack of public sector cash mean that the gasoline-guzzling automobile industry will remain ascendant until well into the next century.

We have heard quite a lot from those who have told us that the automobile is dead, that the future of inner and intra-urban transport will take the form of elevated, computer-controlled walkways, and that the fuel of the future is electricity. The year 2000 is still dangled in front of us as some sort of watershed where suddenly the sensible future takes over from the rather daft present, where the polluting sins of our fathers will be expunged, and we'll all move forward into a better tomorrow. Well, I've got some bad news and some bad news...which would you like first?

It just isn't going to be like that. The vehicles we will be driving, riding in and being transported in by the next century have already taken shape in the planning departments of the automobile giants. The fuel they'll be running on is already determined. The death of the automobile, to coin a phrase, has been greatly exaggerated. And the petrochemical giants are resting easy in their beds in the knowledge that good old gasoline will continue to gush forth into the tanks of these futuremobiles in the way it has for the last century.

There are two major controlling factors in all of this: money and legislation. Legislation is one of the few things that can actually change the way we travel and the fuel we burn. But legislation is made by governments who also benefit hugely from the sale of fossil fuels, just as they do from the sale of tobacco or alcohol. The gas giants know this, as do the car manufacturers, which is why the automobile lineup of 1994 looks much the same as 1993: no sudden electrical revolution; plenty of concept cars in the motor shows with fancy hybrid and electric capabilities, but precious little out there on the road.

When the legislators in California dictated that, by the year 2000, five per cent of all vehicles sold in the state would have to possess non-polluting powerplants, Detroit and the others started to take things a little bit more seriously. A few short years in which to get real about alternative propulsion systems. The problem with this was that ten years is a very short time in the motor industry; so short, in fact, that most of the manufacturers realised that they only had one choice open to them – electric cars.

Waiting around for a recharge

Now, electric cars are funny old things. They rely on the storage of energy, generally, in batteries. Batteries are heavy, expensive, and pretty hopeless when it comes to rapid recharging. Battery technology, although developing all the time, is developing far slower than the vehicle manufacturers would like. If the battery technology remains heavy and expensive, then so will the cars they serve. With petrol or diesel, you can refuel in the twinkle of an eye; with electric, you have to sit around awhile. For instance, the Citella concept, developed by Citroen, has a super-fast recharge system which will provide you with about 20 miles worth of juice in 19 minutes (the amount of time it takes the average Parisian to knock back a couple of pastis). Hardly quick. But the media has it in its head that this is how we are all going to be moving around in the near future.

So what happens? We get our new generation of low-emission, silent ecomobiles, with their preferential parking dispensations and charging infrastructures and everything is just fine. Or is it? Provide a better car and people will be more inclined to use it, *especially* if there are lots of financial and legal perks to go with it. To refer to some Henley Centre for Forecasting data, car ownership, especially two-three car family ownership, is expected to rise continuously into the foreseeable future and the last thing that is going to slow that down is a relaxation on private vehicle use. Electric vehicles will cost more to make (some say twice as much, especially if there is a petrol/diesel generator on board).And if they use the mains to charge themselves up, they'll just push the greenhouse effect further down the line unless we start using a lot more non-fossil fuels in our power stations, like nice clean nuclear power for instance. So let's get real, shall we? The only way to reduce dependence on the car is to replace the benefits it creates with more attractive alternatives. And to do that effectively we have to strip the car down to its psychological essentials and study not what it means to us all today, but what it is *going* to mean in the next ten years or more. Put simply, whatever we like about our car at the moment, we're going to like a whole lot more in the future. Prometheus and Drive[1] are going to make sure that information technology, computer-guidance and integrated communication facilities turn that bucket of bolts into a regular flightdeck. The major comtech organisations are going to ensure that your every fax, telephone, vidcon and two-way computer link requirement is there at your service as the digital GSM Pan-European Cellular network comes on line in the next few years. All this, and in your second, eco-friendly electrical family CityHopper *as well.*

This is nuts! What do real people use their cars for in cities? Picking up a week's shopping for the family (try doing that on a bus). Taking their children to school. Leisure.

If we take a sidelong glance at Europe's demographic shift over the next 10 years, what do we see? More old people, more little children and a nice flat slump where the young adults used to be (those are the ones you see flying around the city on bicycles, by the way). A heavy increase in women going back to work and a couple of other little twists to boot.

It is sad but true: the car companies know that the car isn't going to go away; the petrochemical giants know they're not going to go away; and everyone else from Siemens to Matsushita knows it too. They've all got their futures to think about as well, you know. Now this doesn't mean that the electric car is hopeless; it just means that it has a specific place in the new hierachy of vehicles. A recent management report issued internally within a major petro chemical giant suggested that the electric car will be, for a very long time, a *second* car in the family, and that for medium and long-haul applications, the petrol and diesel vehicle will hold sway into the foreseeable future. Sad as this may seem, this is a realistic assessment.

It is not just the fault of car and gas manufacturers either. A recent study by the Henley Centre for Forecasting suggests that the price of petrol would have to increase *fourfold* before the average car driver would seriously consider giving up his or her car. We've taken the concept of the automobile to our hearts so totally that it's going to take more than guilt to wean us off it.

The need for public and private co-operation

Where does public transport come into all this? Well, my view may be more jaundiced than most, but the three major public transport projects that my consultancy Seymour Powell has been involved in over the last four years – the InterCity 250 high-speed train, the new London Underground Northern Line rolling stock, and the Hankyu suburban rail rolling stock development in Japan – have all ground to a halt for the same reason. No bucks, no Buck Rodgers. Nobody would question the value of such projects. The public transport sectors are still, by and large, the responsibility of governments to fund at national or regional level. But as global recession continues to bite, these expensive programmes are often the first to get the chop. The truth is that there isn't the money circulating any more in the discretionary funding coffers to allow these 'citizencentric' developments to take place.

So, what is to be done? Dwindling public resources and the vested interests of industry pointing in the wrong direction? There are ways ahead....but the watchword is *co-operation*. BMW has formed a relationship with the city that supports it, Munich, to move things forward in a practical and positive way. The new concept embraces all forms of transport, both public and personal, and strives to integrate them in the most practical and efficient way for all users.

Cars circulate on specifically designated routes in a carefully planned system which allows drivers to get close to their destinations and then park-up in ultra-compact, computer-controlled paternoster parking stacks, for which the absolute minimum real estate is required. Efficient tram and bus systems then permit drivers and pedestrians to find their way to their ultimate destinations. Bicycle and motorcycle use is thoughtfully allowed for, often using different routes.

There is nothing new in the elements of this co-operation between motor manufacturer and city council; it is the fact that it is being put into practice that makes the difference. One of the planners working on the scheme referred to it as the 'neurone', a system of co-operative management where all the vested interests are represented. Each transport mode has its place in the system and is used at its best. Electric vehicles are also provided for in the scheme, as and when they come on stream. The system enables and facilitates the introduction of such new transport formats, whilst putting the needs of the community first. Commerce and government working together for the community. Now you're talking.

The 'neurone' engineers are also involved in the development of superior 'termini', the points where users can swap from one system to another. These aren't just smelly, bleak, park'n'ride points, but pleasant, efficient, 'multi-modal' neurones, which provide everything the traveller could desire, from vehicle rental points, stations and parking to shopping and postal facilities. The idea is that they will be so nice that you'll *want* to use them. Simple, isn't it?

Putting desirable alternatives in place

It's no good telling a mother of three that she'll have to do the shopping without her car unless you provide a system that replaces it. It's no good telling the executive in his limo that he will have to give up his in-car telecommunications network and sit on a crowded bus; he will do everything he can to ensure he doesn't have to. It's no good telling a consumer that he has to give up his gas-guzzler if a viable, *desirable* alternative isn't already in place. Legislation is a blunt instrument. The Munich example shows the way ahead. And where does the designer come into all of this? Strangely enough, he is the one component in the whole mix who is actually trained for change, who can facilitate an improved perspective on these issues by showing how people can be put first, without destroying the planet in the process.

References

1. Initiatives taken by vehicle manufacturers in the area of vehicle control and information technology.

Learning from the USSR

Yuri Soloviev RUSSIA

Born in Russia in 1920, **Yuri Soloviev** has practised as an industrial, transport and furniture designer. Between 1945-56, he was the founder and Chief Designer of the Architectural and Art Bureau at the Ministry for Transport Industry, Moscow. Later he founded and acted as Director of the USSR Research Institute of Industrial Design. Soloviev's important works include atomic submarines and icebreakers as well as rail carriage designs. Soloviev now lives in England.

Scientific and technological progress can damage as well as enhance the quality of life – as the mistakes of the Soviet Union, where technical specialists ruled the roost, have demonstrated. Achieving an improvement in material and cultural standards requires a more holistic approach to design.

To speak about the future, it is important not to forget the past. Let us try to recollect how it all started. Design in its modern meaning began to develop with the evolution of industry when mass production became possible. The role of design was enhanced by rapid development of cities and its attendant social change which required the construction of new types of buildings, and the creation of new vehicles, products and equipment.

Engineers started creating objects with new functions. However the new products mostly lacked the essential aesthetic touch, resulting in spiritual deprivation among users. That is why engineers asked artists to beautify the results of their work. It soon became clear, however, that artistic improvement might only be achieved by improving the construction of the product itself. But as a rule, the artist was not able to do that because of his lack of an engineering background. A new specialist was demanded – the designer.

By the 1920s industrial design had become a profession. But 70 years on, what is the future of our profession? Will it have its own renaissance? Or will it contribute to a more general economic renaissance on a global scale? Before answering these questions, let us look around.

Life on earth is more and more affected by science, technology and industry. Even in places where there is no industry, its fruits influence human life. Sophisticated tools, modern transport and communications systems are used in the most distant parts of the world. We are literally overloaded with information. By the end of this century the amount of human knowledge will double, and information flow will be 30 times stronger. Each year professional magazines introduce more than 300,000 inventions and discoveries. Never before has the flow of technologies and structural innovation been so intensive. Never before has it inspired such dynamic changes of lifestyle.

In future, technological progress will continue to determine the quality of life. But technological development not only generates wealth, it also causes destruction. More plants and animals have been destroyed in this century than during all the previous history of civilisation. Much of what industry produces does not correspond to real human needs. It pollutes the environment and leads to waste of natural resources. Mankind is endangered by irrevocable processes: pollution of our air and water, and destruction of our flora and fauna. Our sense of cultural well-being is also frustrated, as universal technology levels the material environment of people and leads to a loss of national traditions and different cultures.

Dangers of the one-sided specialist

Most important decisions are taken on the basis of recommendations by particular specialists, and this has negative consequences for scientific and technological development. Experts are essential because they assure scientific and technological progress, but their recommendations are usually one-sided. I saw an amusingly clear explanation of a particular specialist phenomenon at a New Year party at the design office of the Soviet airplane maker Ilyushin. There were several departments in the design office, each responsible for a particular task: one for the engine, another for the wings, a third for the undercarriage, and so on. At that time the office was working on the passenger IL project. A series of sketches showed how each department viewed the plane. The engine department saw it as a big engine with little wings and miniature passenger compartment. The undercarriage department imagined it with 20 big wheels, a small engine, undeveloped wings, and a very small passenger cabin. Each of the experts had his own image of a plane. In the nineteenth century, a famous Russian humourist Kozma Pryoutkov wrote: 'An expert is like a gumboil: he is one-sided'.

Newsweek magazine recently published an interesting piece about research at the University of California on why there are less geniuses now then in the past. Academic Dean Simonton is certain that the reason is specialisation, which limits the potential for modern geniuses to establish links between different areas of knowledge.

So, should we abandon specialisation? I don't think we should. Progress requires specialisation and profound knowledge. To stop specialisation would be to stop progress. So we find ourselves in a deadlocked situation. An expert is like a gold-digger: the deeper he gets under the ground, the more treasures he finds and the less are his chances to see other valuable things which are often around. It is important to find a way to escape this deadlock as soon as possible. Growing specialisation of different creative professions is an obstacle on the road to achieving harmony in this world – with negative cultural, psychological, social and ecological consequences.

A new relationship between nature and technology

I shall give an example to support this. The Volga, the great Russian river which used to be the main waterway of the nation for centuries, was blocked by a number of electric power stations – in accordance with the recommendations of specialists. The result is that the river, once full-flowing, turned into a swamp in many parts. Fish practically disappeared and the life of people living in cities and villages along the banks changed a lot. It was calculated much too late that the value of black caviar, sterlet and sturgeon lost because of this construction policy was several times greater in value than the electric energy generated by the power stations. This is an example from the Soviet Union, but I am sure that many similar cases might be found in other countries.

As we face a new century it is necessary to find a new relationship between people, technology and nature. People should learn to create products and environments in harmony with the natural habitat, which respond to the requirements of social justice and contribute to the cultural development and prosperity of nations. So complex is the problem that it is recognised in many countries that a new generation of specialist is needed. He or she should not only possess a technical or economic background, but a culturally strategic way of thinking as well. He should be in a position to examine the problem critically and develop integrated, efficient and aesthetically valuable solutions.

I believe the specialist most appropriate for these requirements is a designer. To my mind, a real designer should not only be a talented artist but have a good engineering training. He or she should also be able to combine achievements and discoveries in different areas of knowledge, and have the ability to preview potential consumer expectations in the future. I am convinced that, in the twenty-first century, designer and architect will be key figures in creating the human world, and that both professions shall eventually converge. At the same time I realise perfectly well that some designers and many representatives of other professions might consider these statements too ambitious, especially as they come from a designer. So I want to illustrate my thesis with a story from my experience and let sceptics decide which specialist might be best-equipped to lead complex projects in the future.

A tale from Tbilissi

The story happened in Georgia, a former republic of the Soviet Union. I used to go there in the autumn for my holidays to a lonely and very beautiful place on the Black Sea. On my way there I stopped in Tbilissi, capital of Georgia. One of the branches of my USSR Institute of Industrial Design was located there. Tbilissi was in a state of excitement. An architectural project to develop a new district for 17,000 people in the capital had just been given the go-ahead.

I must tell you that I love Tbilissi. This green southern city is full of charm, with its beautiful houses built mostly at the end of the last century. Naturally, I wanted to see the project. I saw it and was shocked. It was designed in very poor International Style, with primitive 16-floor towers which are seen, to my regret, everywhere in the world. I told my Georgian friends that if they built this development, it would damage their national traditions. I was told that nothing could be done: the project had been approved by Shevardnadze who had already gone on vacation.

You probably know this name. Edward Shevardnadze was the last USSR Minister of Foreign Affairs. At that time he was the First Secretary of the Communist Party of Georgia and a man of unlimited power in the republic.

There was no way I could help, so I went on my holiday. When I arrived at the place, I discovered that Shevardnadze was spending his holiday there as well. We had met before, but at this resort he was always isolated from the 20 or so other people staying there by his security guards, so a serious conversation was not possible.

However, I noticed that Shevardnadze used to swim quite far into the sea alone, leaving his guards on the shore. I decided to share his company. Swimming far in the sea with him alone, I tried to explain how his decision endangered the national culture, how a new district with such poor architecture was impossible for a city with such a strong historical image.

On the third day in the sea, he asked for my suggestion on what to do. I said that if he would stop this project for two months, I would present an alternative project concept for the new development in the best national traditions of Georgia. He agreed. I decided to organise an ICSID Interdesign seminar. As the initiator of this form of brainstorming, I knew how efficient it could be. Fifteen Soviet and fifteen foreign designers, architects and artists were invited to my Tbilissi branch office to participate in the event. I invited Pierre Vago, the brillian French architect and designer, to lead the seminar. After two weeks of intensive and fascinating work, a project concept preserving the best national traditions was prepared. No houses in the project were higher than four floors. Each had a green courtyard inside the building. However the number of residents to be housed remained the same and the cost of construction was even reduced.

All the necessary elements for comfortable life in the district were provided – transport links, schools, hospitals, shops, and so on. The project was received with enthusiasm by the capital's community. Shevardnadze also liked it a lot. He cancelled his previous decision, approved our project and issued a special governmental decree to implement the project.

You might tell me that this was a typical architectural job, nothing new. Not so. It was a new type of architectural project, a complex design task for the twenty-first century. It indicated the direction the design profession might take in the future. I do not consider such work to be perfect. However it reflects my conviction that, in the twenty-first century, designers will head complex projects since they can integrate the developments of science, technology and art.

But to achieve this position, designers must remember that their whole activity should be focused on elevating the material and cultural standards of human life, preserving natural wealth and developing the best national traditions. In this context, our schools of design face a new and very important task. They should prepare broadly educated and by all means talented experts. Leonardo da Vincis are needed for a Renaissance – the more, the better.

Epilogue
Christopher Frayling

In trying to summarise this huge, complex, maddening and stimulating congress into the few words at my disposal, I thought at first of using the 'Renaissance' theme. After all, there were references to Ghiberti's Bapistry Gates in Florence, to Leonardo da Vinci, and to 'latter-day Medicis' as patrons. So I was working towards the idea of the 1980s as the Middle, or Dark, Ages, followed by touching base and pushing things forward in an enlightened way in the 1990s 'Renaissance'.

But, as the congress itself progressed, this idea seemed to work less and less well. Some delegates suggested 'Rococo' or 'Baroque' as more appropriate concepts. 'Going for Baroque' was one alternative title! The point being that 'Baroque' represented the 'Dionysiac Principle' – joy, rather than scientism and reductionism. Others suggested 'the Enlightenment' – with latter-day Diderots and d'Alemberts compiling huge, encyclopaedic design databases. But that, too, was thought by many to be too reductive and scientist. Above all, the 'Renaissance' concept didn't seem to fit, because one major theme of the congress was that the situation designers find themselves in today is not 're-' anything – re-naissance, re-surgence, re-action or whatever. It is a combination of circumstances which are unique to the 1990s.

Take, for example the presentation by Jordi Montana, which stressed *the new* – not in a Modernist way, but in a 'now' way. The Congress explored new consumer habits – a search for symbolic content in products, and for quality, not quantity; new technologies – the drift to customisation; new environmental concerns – the 3 'rs', reduce, recycle, retrieve; new government responsibilities – contextual rather than nationalistic, as Erskine Childers reminded us; and new and urgent global problems – centres of affluence, centres of poverty. On the whole it has been about 'the new' – not about a re-tread at all.

This idea of 'Design Re-naissance' reminds me of Walter Gropius' famous rallying-cry in the 1919 Bauhaus manifesto – the one with the Feininger woodcut of a cathedral on the cover: 'architects, sculptors, painters, we must all turn to the crafts....together let us conceive and create the new building of the future'. Now this rallying-cry has always been mistranslated into English as 'architects, sculptors, painters, we must all *return* to the crafts'. As if designers were supposed to enter the modern era by going backwards. He didn't say *return*. He said turn. This Congress seems to be saying not Re-naissance, but Naissance.

What is being born – as opposed to being reborn – here? One of the key themes has been a strong sense of what *should* be done – and a strong sense of what is being done – and the fluid and sometimes strained relationship between the two. On the one level, a high moral tone; on the other, the pragmatic day-to-day life of the designer. In a sense it is a bit like that last 'Which shall it be?' sequence in *Things to Come,* a film shown to congress delegates. 'We are such small creatures', says one. 'You won't get any where by being modest', implies the other.

If the great 1970s theme was design for need, and the great 1980s theme was design for profit, what in short might be the great 1990s theme? Or are 'great themes', like 'grand narratives', out of fashion, as Jean Claude Garcias suggested? I have identified some themes, more modest themes perhaps, which have emerged. And which have shown that you can get places by being modest:

- The designer as renaissance person – away from hyper-specialisation, towards a broad range of skills: aesthetic, cultural, technological, social, scientific and political.
- The designer as aware of the full implications of design, both within organisations and within society – not just the implications for the American and European sector, but for everyone else as well.
- A suspicion of big stories, big solutions, big ideas: these are fine as a belief system, but the important thing is to build bridges between science fiction and design fact.
- A new global context – from the points of view of social concern, market opportunity, and changing centres of gravity.
- A sense of chaos out there – chaotic information flow, chaotic stockpiling of products, a chaotic market, chaotic government policies, a chaotic pace of change and the key role of the designer as 'a guide to the perplexed', to use Schumacher's phrase, as a kind of gate-keeper.
- A sense that this is a time for taking stock – for linking ethics in some way with aesthetics. But unlike the high-minded Victorians who were also obsessed with ethics, it is also a time when we need to earn our livings in an increasingly fraught environment. William Morris was, it has been estimated, one of the hundred wealthiest men in England. Very few of us have that advantage.
- Above all, a suspicion of all forms of separation, and a strong urge to integrate or cohere; where cities are concerned, not separate zones; where designers are concerned, not separate disciplines and skills, but strategies and convergencies; where the big stories are concerned, not by seeing them as separate and remote, but by starting by changing ourselves and our practices in small ways; where the global context is concerned, not by separating the map into 'centres of affluence' living off the rest, but, as Erskine Childers put it, communicating the idea of one world with a plethora of problems; and where design methods and procedures are concerned, not linear problem-solving, but convergent thinking, or bringing things together.

It is an impossible task to summarise the many sessions, debates and visions of the future at Design Renaissance in a single word or phrase. There were 101 different talks and papers over four days. But it is clear that when market considerations happen to coincide with social concerns – as in Roger Coleman's 'Age: the challenge for design' presentation – then there is broad agreement. So, instead of design for need and design for profit, what do we have? Design for integration? Too clumsy. Design for convergence? Too complicated. Design matters? Certainly, but it is circular. Matters to whom? One theme of the Congress has been that we are better at talking to each other, than to non-specialists, whose images of designers come from the mass-media. Maybe we can settle for design for the quality of life, or design connects, both of them phrases which emerged on the first day of the congress. Or, better still, design for people.

Two moments from Design Renaissance will stick in my mind for a long time. One is Victor Papanek quoting in discussion Charles Rennie Mackintosh, who said 'there is hope in honest error, none in icy perfection'. The other is Yuri Soloviev's story about persuading Edward Shevardnadze not to go ahead with a dreadful town planning scheme in Georgia, while swimming out into the Black Sea, on holiday. I guess the moral of the tale is: if you are up to your neck in it – keep talking, keep persuading, grab the moment when it comes, have a healthy disregard for bureaucracy, and be a strong swimmer. Oh, and as you are swimming, try not to lose your bearings and always remember that the word 'utopia' means 'of no place at all'.

Design Renaissance has certainly provided some great discussion topics; it has been at times an invigorating experience and it has even swum out into some uncharted waters. Quite an achievement, on this huge scale.

About the Chartered Society of Designers

The Chartered Society of Designers is the professional body representing the interests of designers in the UK. Its function is to promote high standards of design, to foster professionalism and to emphasise designers' responsibility to society, to the client and to each other.

The Society was granted a Royal Charter in 1976. Membership is a recognised professional qualification. The Society currently represents more than 7,000 individual members and undertakes a full programme of lobbying, design promotion and conferences, awards, events and publications.

The Society was founded in 1930, and in the decades since then has acted as a focus for the best of British design talent. Its mission remains unchanged: to provide leadership within the design profession; to set and maintain professional standards; and to demonstrate the role of design in wealth creation and improving the quality of life.

Design Review

Design Review is the quarterly journal of the Chartered Society of Designers. Published in association with Wordsearch Ltd (publishers of magazines including *Blueprint, Eye* and *Tate*) it brings together comment and analysis on all aspects of design from around the world. *Design Review* is available on subscription to non members from the Society at the address below.

Business Design Programme

The Business Design Programme is a new initiative established to strengthen the dialogue between the design profession and companies in business and industry. It aims to help design users to recognise and develop opportunities where strong management of design can make a major contribution to profitability and business success.

The Business Design Programme offers a wide range of benefits to member companies including an intensive and well-researched calendar of seminars, talks and discussions; access to privileged information and research; membership of a powerful and active body for lobbying policy-makers and opinion-formers; and full company membership of the CSD.

Founder members include: Andry Montgomery, Arjo Wiggins, BAA, BT, Business Design Centre, Emess, William Grant & Sons, Haworth UK, IBM, London Regional Transport, Marks & Spencer, Pearce Signs, TSB, Voko, Volvo Car and Wood and Wood International. For further information on membership of the Business Design Programme, please contact the Development Director at the address below.

The Minerva Awards

The Minerva Awards are the CSD's leading forum for recognition of professional excellence. Awards are made annually in the categories of Environmental, Product and Graphic Design as well as Design Management. Shortlisted projects in each category are published in each issue of *Design Review,* and winners announced in late May of each year.

For further information please write to: The Minerva Awards, c/o *Design Review,* 26 Cramer Street, London W1M 3HE, United Kingdom.

Membership

Who should join?

The Chartered Society of Designers represents practising designers in all disciplines, design managers, design educators and students on recognised full time design courses. If you practice design, the Society offers the UK's only internationally recognised professional qualification.

How to join.

As a full Member or Fellow: Full Corporate Membership or Fellowship of the Society permits usage of the affix MCSD or FCSD. Membership is granted by assessment. For details of assessment dates (in venues throughout the UK and Hong Kong) and requirements for practitioners in specific design disciplines, please contact the Membership Manager at the address below.

As a Diploma Member: Diploma Membership is open to all designers between the ages of 18 and 30 who have not yet practised design for a sufficient period to qualify for full membership. Membership is granted automatically on application to graduates of all full time design courses recognised by the CSD, who apply within 18 months of graduation. For details, contact the Membership Department. Other candidates may apply through assessment.

As a Student Member: Student Membership is open to all students of CSD recognised design degree and HND courses in the UK. Full details are available from the Membership Department.

The Chartered Society of Designers
29 Bedford Square London WC1B 3EG United Kingdom

Telephone (0)71 631 1510 Facsimile (0)71 580 2338

Design Renaissance
– Congress Speakers

Geoffrey Adams	England	Janice Kirkpatrick	Scotland
Eugene Asse	Russia	Lisa Krohn	USA
Danielle Barr	England	Ian Lang MP	Scotland
David Bayliss	England	Christopher Lorenz	England
Maria Benkzton	Sweden	Ross Lovegrove	England
Pierre Bernard	France	Andy Lowe	England
David Bernstein	England	Ezio Manzini	Italy
Thomas Beucker	Germany	Stefano Marzano	Netherlands
Robert Blaich	USA	Eamon McCabe	England
Karl Deiter Bodack	Germany	Katherine McCoy	USA
Michael Brill	USA	Charles McKean	Scotland
Jose Korn Bruzzone	Chile	Norman McNally	Scotland
Colin Bryce	Scotland	Bill Moggridge	USA/England
Pavel Büchler	Czechoslovakia	Jordi Montana	Spain
	/Scotland	Peter Mowforth	Scotland
Phillip Butta	USA	Takashi Murai	Japan
Dugald Cameron	Scotland	Jeremy Myerson	England
Ken Cato	Australia	Wally Olins	England
Sy Chen	Japan	Victor Papanek	USA
Eskine Childers	Ireland	Peter Phillips	USA
Hazel Clark	Hong Kong	Bernhard Posner	Belgium
Roger Coleman	England	Jane Priestman	England
Liz Conover	USA	Paul Priestman	England
Sir Terence Conran	England	David Puttnam	England
Gillian Crampton Smith	England	Helen Rees	England
Baroness Denton of Wakefield	England	Arthur Rosenblatt	USA
Frank Duffy	England	Gitta Salomon	USA
Gert Dumbar	Netherlands	Vikas Satwalekar	India
Anthony Dunn	England	Paula Scher	USA
Michael Edwardes-Evans	England	Richard Scott	England
Rodney Fitch	England	Tom Scott	USA
Alan Fletcher	England	Chris Seeley	England
Christopher Frayling	England	Serge Serov	Russia
Shigeo Fukuda	Japan	Richard Seymour	England
Toshio Fukuda	Japan	Gordon Sked	England
Ervin Y Galantay	Switzerland	Yuri Soloviev	Russia
Jean Claude Garcias	France	Mads Ravn Sørensen	Denmark
Jeanne Marie Giordano	USA	Wojciech Suchorzewski	Poland
David Gosling	USA	Deyan Sudjic	England
Kenneth Grange	England	Yoichi Sumita	Japan
Stuart Gulliver	Scotland	John Thackara	Netherlands
Sir Graham Hills	Scotland		/England
Eva Jiricna	Czechoslovakia	Ivor Tiefenbrun	Scotland
	/England	Bob Tyrrell	England
Anthony Jones	England	Daniel Weil	England
Tibor Kalman	USA	Paul Williams	England
Shiu Kay Kan	England	Michael Wolff	England
Larry Keeley	USA	John Worthington	England
Derrick de Kerckhove	Canada	James Woudhuysen	England
Tony Key	England	Dan Wright	Scotland
Hiroaki Kimura	Japan	Katsumi Yamatogi	Japan
Perry King	Italy	Peter York	England